TRUST

Are You Kidding?

Pitfalls of the Current Trust System Exposed
How to Establish a Trust that Works!

By: Sue Farley

New York

Trust Are You Kidding?
Pitfalls of the Current Trust System Exposed
How to Establish a Trust that Works!
Copyright 2009 Barbara Suzanne Farley. All rights reserved.

ISBN 978-1-60037-498-2

MORGAN · JAMES
THE ENTREPRENEURIAL PUBLISHER

Morgan James Publishing, LLC
1225 Franklin Ave., STE 325
Garden City, NY 11530-1693
Toll Free 800-485-4943
www.MorganJamesPublishing.com

In an effort to support local communities, raise awareness and funds, Morgan James Publishing donates one percent of all book sales for the life of each book to Habitat for Humanity. Get involved today, visit **www.HelpHabitatForHumanity.org**.

DEDICATION

To my esteemed colleagues

ACKNOWLEDGMENTS[1]

I first want to acknowledge Ernest Freeman, a brilliant technologist who has worked with me for six years developing technology that will change the trust and estate industry;

To Michael Besack, an enterprise system technologist who assisted in the design of sophisticated architecture to transform an industry resistant to change;

To Ed Frey, a talented business operations consultant, who saw the risk to the industry in remaining where it is;

To Larry Allen who tried to convince an intransigent industry to change, and to Peter Myers Esq. a gifted estate planner for his input.

Thank you for all the thousands of hours we have spent together trying to solve what many advised could not be done. It can be done, and it is being done.

1   Ernest Freeman 30+ yrs System architecture design, knowledge systems
        Borland, Caltech; Michael Besack 30+ years distributed multi-tiered
        architecture design, B2B supply chain mgmt, UC Berkeley; Edward Frey
        15 yrs strategy and business operations consultant, 8 yrs growth company,
        MIT, HBS; Larry Allen 30+ years Financial Services Harvard, HBS; Peter
        Myer Esq. American University, UC Hastings

CONTENTS

PART THREE

Take Matters Into Your Own Hands: It's Up to Us to Solve Our Trust Problems

INTRODUCTION
Your Money is Not Safe

One morning nearly twenty-five years ago, I arose after five hours of sleep to prepare for an eighteen to nineteen hour day. I said a prayer. I prayed to remember the evidence code and to make the proper objections. I prayed that my papers were in order and that the witnesses would show up as planned. I was about to go to court over mismanagement of a trust, a document that sets up someone to be in charge of your money when you die or if you become incapacitated. I was up against one of the nation's biggest and most respected banks that had hired two of the most prestigious and powerful law firms against me and my client. I ate nothing because my nerves would not allow me to digest any food.

Up to this point in my career, I had five years of trial experience, hence my assignment of the case. But, I won't kid you; I was shaking in my boots. It was just me and my associate lawyer standing against a wall of money and power on behalf of a group of people who, in good faith, had named this prestigious bank as the entity in charge of their trust.

The case was overwhelming. I was no stranger to some of the awful things that could happen in a dispute over money. My father left me as a child, and my mother and grandmother fought him in the courts for years to pay back-child support. They eventually won, but it was emotionally and financially devastating for us all. It was one of the reasons I became a lawyer. I wanted to make sure that what happened to my mother would never happen to me.

As I made my opening statements back in 1983, I couldn't help thinking of what I had learned. Here was a prominent San Francisco family, one of the city's largest and most respected retailers, who claimed the bank's administration defrauded them and lost money from their trust. The family claimed that the trust should be replenished with the less than $50,000 the bank had lost. They also claimed that the bank should not be paid trustee's fees for its poor performance and should be removed as trustee.

At first I was struck by the thought, "Why would anyone have to sue the very person or entity placed in a position of trust in charge of a family's assets?" I initially concluded it must simply be bad blood between the two parties and that this was a unique case. I couldn't have been more wrong.

When I first picked up the file and started to review it, I found that it was a fraud and breach of trust action that had been filed by the managing partner of my firm against a major bank on behalf of the heirs to the patriarch's fortune. When I interviewed the heirs, the patriarch's daughter and grandchildren, I was told that for many years the bank had treated the family with disdain. The bank had been hired to manage the family trust, but it consistently refused to answer their questions or give them documents regarding management and decisions made on their behalf. The bank had tried to establish a "depreciation reserve" claiming two things: the family store in San Francisco—a much loved and beautiful part of the San Francisco downtown landscape—was a depreciating asset which would require replacement at some time in the future, and money from the trust would be withheld from the beneficiaries to fund a replacement building. That seemed to me simply a reason to withhold funds from the family. What made it worse was that the beneficiaries were also questioning whether the lease was being enforced. They had no proof the rent was being properly collected from the store as payments were based on a complicated lease requiring percentages of the sales in certain departments—notably the antique, lamp, and jewelry sections—be added to the lease payments.

The law firm I was up against was one of the largest firms in San Francisco with several hundred lawyers and represented many major corporate clients. It was reputed for being tough. But while I might not have had prestige on my side, I had the law and facts on my side. I spent time reviewing correspondence retained by the heirs, and through it I saw a pattern of non-responsive answers to questions and even those were unreasonably delayed. Each of the beneficiaries had their own tales to tell of the arrogance, misdirection, and refusal to respond to their inquiries and requests. Perhaps most egregious was the bank's refusal to make distributions. The bank had also filed its accounting in the court, and the beneficiaries objected to the fees and charges claiming the bank had mismanaged their accounts. Basically the family had reached its limit and united against this bank.

This was wild. This case went against everything I knew about trusts and estates. In simple terms, a trust is a relationship in which a person, called a trustor or a grantor, transfers something of value, called an asset, to another person, called a trustee. The trustee, the person named by the grantor, is to oversee the management and distribution of funds, and holds, manages, and controls this asset—any kind of property, including money—for the benefit of the grantor or a third person. A beneficiary is the person receiving the funds of the trust. Most important, the trust is a separate legal entity from the grantor. My background from law school in trusts and estates told me the trustee owed an undivided duty of loyalty to the beneficiaries. The trustee had a duty to communicate and disclose all that was happening with the trust's money and to represent and promote the beneficiary's interests in all matters. The trustee, by law, had a duty to account and report on its actions, a duty of service to its beneficiaries, a duty of honesty. This was a bank that had long held itself out to the public as a professional—and therefore trusted—trustee. How could it be that all the beneficiaries were complaining of the same things?

The bank's counsel and I met and began discussing the case. I asked if there was some way of settling the matter. I said I had reviewed the file and found the claims of my clients had merit, and that the bank should pay back the money it had lost and the case would go away. The bank's lawyers responded that the beneficiaries owed the bank money for back-trustee fees. (This was before the fees were automatically deducted from the account, when the beneficiaries actually had to approve the fees before they were paid.) I said, "Why would we pay the bank for mismanaging the assets and losing trust money?" They didn't like that and answered me with a threat that they would recover the bank's unpaid fees, and the trust would pay for their attorney fees and costs in doing so. I was appalled. Could they do this? I found out yes, they could. I thought it odd that the bank would not have settled this case as the family was prominent and the bank should not want the adverse publicity of such a challenge. But I kept my opinion to myself and simply said I did not think we were talking about the same case. The meeting concluded.

The lawyer's threat of recovering their attorney fees and costs from my client's trust was a real one. The law allows a trustee to defend itself from challenge by the beneficiaries at the trust's expense. I figured I had better bone up on trust law before this went to court. I began reading everything I could find on trusts. Treatises, volumes of reference books, and case law; I inhaled it all. I wanted to know what the opposing firm had that made them so arrogant. They were professionals. They were in the business, after all. Surely they knew a lot more than I did. As I read the volumes of books and case analyses, I continued to come up with one conclusion: I should win this case.

I needed to see the bank's file of the family trust. I sent the bank interrogatories (documents with questions asking for support of the bank's position) so I could see the bank's records to determine if the claims were supported by anything other than my client's word. I was met with stonewalling. Few if any documents were produced, and the interrogatories were objected to. In every instance I had to enlist the court's orders to compel the bank's compliance in answering my questions and giving me the documents. When the bank finally provided documents, I found that other documents had been withheld. The bank refused to send these additional documents asserting they were subject to the attorney-client privilege. This really incensed me. If the bank was acting on behalf of the beneficiaries, and the trust was paying the bank's legal bills, the documents would not be subject to any confidential privilege because the lawyers and bank were supposed to be working for my clients. *But* if the bank was paying its personal lawyers for its own benefit with trust money, then it would have to justify why the trust was paying the bill. Up until the time of the dispute, the bank was supposed to be acting on behalf of my client; after the dispute it was entitled to retain its own lawyers to defend itself. I should have been able to see all documents relating to the decisions made by the bank on my client's behalf. Even if the lawyers were advising the bank, I was entitled to see the documents. After more court hearings, I won this battle and the bank had to produce its files.

By this time, things started getting ugly. The bank demanded the depositions of all the plaintiffs (the family I was representing), and I in turn demanded the depositions of the bank officers who had spanned a ten- to fifteen-year period of administration. The bank hired a second law firm with equally impressive credentials as the first, and over one hundred more lawyers from this new firm joined an already legion of lawyers in the defense. Things were getting ludicrous. The claim was for less than $50,000; why wouldn't the bank just pay it? The bank would spend at least twenty times that in defending the litigation. But there was no settlement, and the only rationale I could come up with as to why was that the bank knew that if it lost, its conduct would be scrutinized more closely. It was either that or the bank was trying to teach my client and others a lesson not to question or challenge its conduct. I figured that by hiring high-powered law firms and pouring hundreds of thousands of dollars into the case, the bank was trying to bury me and my client in a mountain of papers, motions, and expenses so that the case would simply be forgotten, and "business as usual" would prevail.

What the bank didn't count on was my indignation at what I saw as an injustice, arrogance, and abuse of power. I dug in my heels and we fought. Many of the bank witnesses had retired or were not anxious to testify. They had to be found, subpoenaed, and deposed. It was like getting yardage in a football game; every inch was hard fought. I discovered the bank was not enforcing the lease on the family store. It never challenged the amount it received from the tenant, and it did not check on the percentages owed. In other words, it ignored the terms and conditions of the lease. The language in the trust also required that the trustee make periodic visits to the store to ensure the property was well kept. The bank's officers decided that they could visit the store and shop at the same time; in fact, the store was only visited when bank officers were shopping. I questioned trust officer after trust officer, and it didn't matter. Year after year and trust officer to trust officer, the answer was the same. They had never analyzed the lease, had never established a method for determining the propriety of payments, had never really checked whether what was collected was correct, and had just reported what they received.

So why was this bank not enforcing the lease? I suspected because they were also soliciting business from the lessee, but the court said there was insufficient evidence to prove this conflict. As I delved further into the case, I found multiple areas where the bank simply failed to perform at a professional level. The bank's only response to the beneficiaries' inquiries was threats of additional fees and charges to the trust to handle the inquiries. The bank threatened that any challenge would come out of my client's pocket because the bank's attorneys would be paid from the trust. In other words, the beneficiaries would be paying for both sides of any challenge.

The battle raged for four years, and we finally went to trial. The trial spanned three to four months. My associate and I presented our case in the day and worked into the wee hours of the morning preparing motions, evidentiary challenges, briefs, examination and cross examination for the next day. I could not hold down my food as I was so stressed. I lost ten pounds in the trial, dropping to 108 lbs. But through the trial process, I finally got to see what the lawyers had, what had made them so arrogant, what they had refused to give me under the attorney client privilege. *They had nothing.* It was what made them lose their case. When the lawyers were confronted with the facts: the years of neglect by the bank; the indifference of the trust officers; the disguised excuses why distributions were not forthcoming; and the bank's rationale for their failed performance, the legions of attorneys had nothing to say in their defense except that it was the way the bank did business. I argued for punitive damages because the bank had misled the public and my client into believing that it operated professionally. The bank certainly charged as professionals, but it had performed as a rank amateur. I asked for $1 million and got it. When we won the case, I was not ecstatic; I was not proud that I had brought down such a powerful entity. Instead I was exhausted and relieved as I thought the bank would perform better and other beneficiaries would benefit from a changed system. As I will discuss throughout this book, I was wrong.

I was surprised the case hit the press. Usually winning a case means it appears in the lawyer journals and lawyer reports, but that's about it. This case hit the *SF Chronicle,* the *Wall St. Journal,* and the *LA Times* among other newspapers and publications. I had touched a nerve in an industry cloaked in secrecy and family wealth. I had stumbled into an arena where control over wealth and power over families sometimes meant mismanagement, abuse, lack of accountability, frustration, and loss of assets for those caught in the web of trusts and estates.

My phone started to ring off the hook. The next case I handled was for the co-executrix to the estate of an heiress of a mining fortune in San Diego. The co-executrix claimed the financial institution that served as the other co-executor was trying to orchestrate a sale of the land held in the estate to another one of the bank's customers. In this claim, the co-executrix also stated the bank was selling assets in a fire-sale fashion, had not analyzed the tax obligations, ignored her objections to their conduct, and tried to marginalize her input. I won that one too. To my surprise, others had the same problems; I quickly discovered that trusts-gone-bad weren't just a problem of the super-wealthy. I was inundated with requests for help from beneficiaries of more modest trusts—the average is $1.1 million—as well as those who were going to lose the family farm.

I changed firms and headed the litigation department of the San Francisco office of a Los Angeles-based firm. Since my new firm represented financial institutions, I would also get the opportunity to understand the financial institution perspective. I undertook risk analysis looking at how financial institutions view litigation, claims, and defense as a means of resolution. Over the years I have since represented individuals, corporations, and others in just about every capacity in a trust or estate dispute, and it is why I am writing this book. People often do not know what is happening to the money that has been placed in trust. Grantors believe they are protecting their wealth and family by creating trusts, but the industry looks at that same wealth as a way to make a profit. All I can say is if you have or are thinking about creating a trust, under the current system your money is not safe. No matter what your trust says or what the bank or others promises you, you need to look again and think about who is making sure your wishes are honored.

Now you may be thinking, "This is all very disturbing, but it can't possibly pertain to me; I don't have enough assets to put in a trust." That is an all-too-common misconception. We've all heard of "trust-fund babies," those individuals who had a wealthy parent or grandparent who set aside money for them only to squander it away by staying in school forever, or worse, running around the country following *The Grateful Dead* or flaunting themselves in the media. In other words, many of us think that since we don't have that kind of wealth, why should we care? While the prevailing notion is that trusts are thought of as a subject of interest only to the very wealthy, you need to rethink that viewpoint. If you bought a house for $200,000 in 1970, it may now be worth $2,000,000 and yes, that is real money. Furthermore, our stocks and/or retirement funds are producing sizable returns, and many of us, whether we're aware or it or not, have sizable assets. To top it off, more and more of us are inheriting wealth. Even if everything you own adds up to $500,000 or so in assets, trusts are definitely something to consider.

Very simply, the subject of trusts touches us all. The trust industry is a trillion-dollar business (that's twelve zeros, and that's a lot of money!) and so everyone who is in the business of making money wants a part of this very large and lucrative pie. I've seen it happen over and over. Anyone who is a trustee overseeing a million dollars or more is going to make decisions about the trust that will benefit themselves or the institution they represent. The grantors put their undying trust in the people or institutions they name as trustees. The beneficiaries, the people who are supposed to benefit from the trust and who are supposed to be protected by law, lose because they have to sue the trustee if their trust is violated. The trustee is usually given the power to cover the cost of the lawsuit with money from the trust while the beneficiaries don't have this option. So the sheer cost of a lawsuit locks out whole classes of individuals who have rights that have been violated but do not have the funds to pursue them. If they do choose to pursue a case, they run the risk of totally depleting their trust.

With deregulation of our financial institutions, trusts have become profit centers. Investments in trusts are no longer made for the benefit of the beneficiaries alone; they often are made for the beneficiaries only if the investment also benefits the bank. There are conflicts of interest everywhere, and our money, set aside in trusts, is simply not being managed in ways that benefit us. What's worse the smaller your trust, the more you are in danger of falling prey to unidentified investments by the bank and undisclosed fees. It's like the woman whose mother had set aside $100,000 for her in a trust fund when she was fifteen years old. She was supposed to collect the full amount plus interest when she turned twenty-five. When she went to collect, there was nothing left. In the ten years the bank held her trust, the fund was completely consumed by fees, poor investments, and God knows what.

But please don't think you can easily solve this problem by naming a family member or a trusted personal friend as your trustee. While a family member or trusted friend of the family can act responsibly as the trustee, most family trustees don't offer a consistently good alternative because they are not trained as trustees. There are complex accounting and legal requirements in any trust, and family members or friends, no matter how intelligent they may be, simply do not have the training to handle all the complexities a trust demands. They have to make hard decisions about how the money in the trust is being invested and then how it's disbursed. Also personal preferences can play too large a role. Sometimes the personal representative favors certain family members. They can also take family assets, fail to report or account, refuse to respond to questions, and start to treat the funds and assets as their own. When the beneficiaries question the trustee, it becomes a family dispute. I have seen more families break up over trusts than I care to comment on.

Do I have your attention yet? I hope so because I want you to read this book to educate yourself. In short, I want you to learn what I have learned. I want to debunk myths and ideas about trusts so you can ensure your trusts are set up right and your money stays safe so that it really benefits those it intends to benefit—your heirs, not those who are administering the trust. All too often people leave their trusts—their money!— in the hands of their lawyers and banking institutions because they think that trusts are too difficult to comprehend or that they are the "professionals" and they will properly handle it all. Not so. Your estate planner usually will not be around when you die, so won't be able to explain to your trustee what the terms meant or what you intended. Given the way trusts are set up now, your named representative trustee will probably not understand your trust any better than you do. This is so because the language of the trust is often vague and confusing, and fails to tell your administrator *how* to make decisions regarding your assets or how to accomplish the goals you have set. These crucial decisions are left entirely up to the discretion of the trustee or administrator.

Not only do I want to educate you about the problems associated with trusts, I want to present you with some solutions. It's one thing to cry foul; it's another entirely to suggest a way to do something about it. For years I thought the industry would change because of the advances made in technology, both in the sophistication of the software and in the computing power to run it. I kept thinking, "Finally, trust administration can be automated so decisions will be consistent from one trust officer to another and decisions can be tracked and predicted." I was certain that someone at some bank would figure out how the administrative process could be linked to decision making and be responsive to the beneficiaries' needs and demands so answers would be at their fingertips. I truly believed I would find my job as a lawyer having to deal with trusts-gone-bad obsolete. But no, the problems did not change. In fact, from year to year, they have gotten worse. The law still favors trustees, those who are supposed to be neutral caretakers of our funds and families, and has not changed. There is no automation except in the form of sophisticated accounting functions that in part are set up to take fees from your account for the work that may or may not have been done.

So while we have sophisticated ways of tracking the money, we have no way of tracking the decisions behind the numbers. We have no standards against which performance can be measured, except in the broadest sense. We waive our rights regularly to hold our fiduciaries to any standard of accountability but gross negligence. Why is this? Because the banks don't want to change. They make money the way it is. They simply don't have the mechanisms in place to perform the tasks required to administer your trust properly. This is compounded by the fact that you've given them a "broad grant of powers," language in the trust document that allows them to do whatever they please. Once you grant power to a bank—or anyone for that matter—to control your money and there's no one looking over their shoulder, what do you think is going to happen? The bank is going to find ways to invest your money in a manner that also benefits itself. This is a direct conflict of interest and constitutes what's called self-dealing— making decisions that benefit the bank rather than benefiting the beneficiaries it is to serve.

Everyone is at risk in this game. Trusts are mired in the antithesis of trusts—they are not always trustworthy. But the bottom line is I hope you pay attention because it's *your* money!

So not only do I want to educate you, I want you to get angry. I want you to do something about it. Learn what I know about what's wrong with the system and consider the solutions I present in this book. Because of my litigation experience working on both sides of the issue, I have spent a great deal of time and effort learning about and then working to solve the problems that have remained constant throughout my career. I've done it not only because I want to spare my family from these same problems, but I also want to lift the shroud of secrecy that surrounds this trillion-dollar business. I want to provide you with a map for planning and administration so you won't have to deal with the lawsuits, family break-ups, and dysfunction that often result from badly written wills and trusts and their poor administration.

It is time we learned what is involved, how to deal with the issues, and how to protect ourselves, our families, and our estates against the problems that plague the current trust system.

PART ONE
Trusts 101: Knowing the Basics

The issue of estate planning is complicated, even more complicated than your family lawyer makes it out to be. I find that the number one problem in dealing with cases of trusts-gone-bad, whether they concern the beneficiaries or any number of fiduciaries who have been named to take care of the estate or trust, is that those involved in the cases are simply uninformed about all the issues that are at stake (and that includes the banks). Part one is all about the basics. You will find out what trusts are and how they differ from wills, and by the end of part one you'll be aware of some of the various trusts that are available to you. You will also have an idea of the various elements that need to go into planning your estate, elements that your lawyers most likely aren't addressing because they're on the planning side of trusts, not the administrative side. So while your lawyer might not be aware that he or she must take a hard look at how your trust will play out, you will be very aware of what you need to include in your trust to make it work best for you and your beneficiaries.

CHAPTER ONE:

What is a Will and What is a Trust?

Estates take a lifetime to build. An estate is the sum of everything you own as well as all of your liabilities. Since Americans are becoming wealthier, they have more assets to be protected. Americans tend to think they only need to protect their money from Uncle Sam. The most common misconception about trusts is that they are simply a way to minimize taxes on your estate when you die. They are so much more than that. They are a way to provide for your spouse, your children, and even subsequent generations.

Even if you've never considered a trust or thought about estate planning, consider what would happen to you or your family if you died tomorrow. If you think all is well because you already have a will or trust, think again. Today's estate plans, while better than nothing, are simply inadequate to deal with the issues that erupt at death. Will your spouse and your children really be provided for in the way that you want? Is your money well protected from all those who appear at death ready to take what you have left?

The Estate Planning Process

If you've ever had to go through the process of estate planning, you know it is not the most pleasant experience. You are planning for a time after your death and many want to get it over with as soon as possible. You hire an estate planner—no small expense because he or she is always a lawyer. When you walk in, the planner asks you to start talking. You tell him about your family, your assets, and what you want to do about both. The lawyer is listening intently, but he's also making decisions about what kind of trust you need. He's thinking, "This is a QTIP trust with a bypass provision," or a "disclaimer trust," or something else because there are many different ways that he can structure your trust. He's basically thinking about how to best minimize your taxes with the IRS, because that's what he's trained to do. All lawyers have to take at least a semester's worth of trust and estate law, and many schools mandate a year; it's that complicated.

When you leave the lawyer's office, you expect that sometime in the near future he will send you a thick document—your estate plan. You start reading. You may understand some parts of it, but not others. So although you're befuddled by the language, you are either too embarrassed to ask for explanation, you don't want to be charged for the time it takes to explain it, or you assume that the lawyer listened to you and what he's done is in your best interest; he's protected you. You rely on that assumption, and you sign the document and move on. Hiring an estate planner is like hiring a wedding planner and just giving her the date, the amount you want to spend on the wedding, and the location where you want it to take place. If you did that, you would certainly have a wedding, but it would probably be very different from the one you envisioned. The same holds true for estate plans. They take planning and foresight, and they require your involvement.

You need to think about what you want for your children, grandchildren, and heirs. Plan for contingencies in the event they experience major life changes. For example, you may have money set aside for your grandson's college tuition, but what if he wants to start a business instead? What if something happens and he needs long-term care rather than college? While difficult to think about, consider what will happen if your family strays from the plan you've made whether by choice or circumstance.

In addition, you need to plan your own care. According to AARP data, a sixty-five-year-old man today is expected to live to age eighty-one, and a sixty-five-year-old woman is expected to live to age eighty-five. In order to ensure there will be enough money for you to live on, you need to establish mechanisms that will speak for you when you can no longer speak for yourself. That means anticipating events like

Alzheimer's, dementia, surgery or illness. There are simply too many forces and too many people with dismal track records who are willing to relieve others of what they have for you to leave these important decisions to chance.

As has been well documented by the press and as I pointed out earlier, the world of personal finance is changing, requiring more than just a will. So before we get into the nuts and bolts of estate planning, let's look at the other reasons why—even if you don't consider yourself wealthy—you need to worry about estate planning.

Money Isn't the Only Thing that Has Changed

As I mentioned in the introduction, many of us who wouldn't consider ourselves "wealthy" nevertheless have significant assets requiring planning. Because of our sound investments, our solid retirement funds, our savvy about real estate and a host of other asset-generating activities, we're generally building our wealth in a much more productive way than our parents did. However, more wealth is only one of the changes in our world that is affected by estate planning. In addition to earning more than our parents, in many cases we're dealing with more complex families. Complicating the consequences of our increased wealth is the changing structure of our society and families. People are more mobile and families get separated. The 50 percent divorce rate has also expanded the demographics of American families from a core family of mother, father, and children to include stepmothers, stepfathers, stepchildren, stepsisters, and stepbrothers, as well as relatives of each. In addition, we do not always get married. We live together, have short or long-term out-of-marriage relationships, and same-sex partnerships. Children often result from these relationships, and their rights become the subject of dispute and litigation. The parental tree and the family tree may no longer overlay one another because there is a mixture of bloodlines and parental roles. In addition, birth parents may not be genetic parents, and with the advances in reproductive technology, the lines between who is related to whom could blur even more.

These changes have skewed inheritance rights as nontraditional families are growing, and divorce has thrust together people and relations that do not necessarily want to be related. So too, America melds people and cultures from all over the world, and there is no one correct answer as to how the estate plan should be structured. Who inherits from whom, what cultures and traditions dominate, what family values are passed on, and how they fit into an American system presents us with a complicated mosaic of problems that the current way of planning and executing estates simply cannot handle.

Enormous change has also occurred within the institutions charged with managing our estates. They're called "professional fiduciaries," a fancy term for either the bank or trust company that you have chosen to administer your trust. Any fiduciary, whether it is personal or professional, owes a duty of undivided loyalty to the beneficiaries. Our banks have traditionally been the place where we put our trust and confidence in representing our interest and preserving our assets. Up until the very recent past, relationships grew between our businesses and our financial institutions and those relationships in turn fostered a confidence and trust in the individuals with whom we dealt. These individuals were the natural choice as trustee when we created trusts because of our long relationship with them.

This is no longer the case. While financial institutions perform a needed function and have gained the confidence of most of us to provide certain services, the relationships that used to develop over time and that were based on banking relationships and long-term investments is no longer there. The personal relationships we used to develop suffer because bank officers are far more mobile than they were even a generation ago. They leave or move to different divisions within the same institution.

But that's just the tip of the proverbial iceberg. When President Clinton deregulated the banks in the 1990s, the nature of the relationship between the professional fiduciary and the beneficiary changed even more. Up until the deregulation, the trust departments at commercial banks were run independently of other bank operations on the premise that the trustee's judgment was independent of other bank interests and promoted the interests of the beneficiaries over their own. The trust departments of commercial banks were regarded as those with the expertise and investment acumen to preserve the wealth of the rich for generations to come. Changes resulting from deregulation of our financial institutions and the focus on "profit" has changed the focus of the trust departments. Our fiduciaries must now assume the sometimes conflicting roles of money manager, trust salesman, asset manager, and even parent.

Unfortunately, our financial institutions have generally focused on what they do best—money management—even though many try to sell you on the idea that they're giving you personal service. Because they handle thousands of trusts, the people who are handling them, while often well-intentioned, are not trained well enough to do an adequate job as trustee. So your trust really isn't "personally serviced," quite the opposite in fact. It often comes to the bank in several documents. It is reviewed, the assets segregated to different divisions for management, and the document is filed away in the far recesses of the bank never to be looked at again unless there's a problem. The bank has automated the parts of the process that are convenient to them. They automatically deduct their fees every month, and when it comes time to make decisions about what investments need to be made, they are often well within their rights—because you gave them a "broad grant of powers" to invest as they see fit—to invest your money in a way that benefits themselves as much as or more than benefits the trust itself.

As a result of these changes and the dissatisfaction around the service the bank provides, many people are choosing to name a family member or close friend as their trustee because this person is perceived as more responsive to the needs of the family. However, as I warned in the introduction, the personal trustee usually lacks the training and skills necessary to properly perform the tasks. Our banks should be improving their skills and responsiveness and filling this role. It is only when the banks can balance lower cost with greater personal service that they will regain their clients' trust. More and more services are de-personalized as institutions embrace a rapidly changing business model of automated service, yet that service is not for the customer as much as it is to account for the money in the bank's hands.

It is important for all of us to recognize the different roles we expect our named personal representatives to play, and plan for the strengths and weaknesses of the people or institutions we place as administrators of our estates and trusts. The changing environment in commercial banks means a change in the way our trusts are administered by our trustees. More and more, we need to make informed decisions regarding exactly what we are getting for the money we spend. We must take responsibility for whole areas in our lives where we used to rely on others to promote our interests ahead of their own. Just as service stations no longer pump our gas for us, there are fewer and fewer people or institutions that are willing to take care of our assets and families for us.

The Effects of Bad Planning

In order to take more responsibility for the way our estates and trusts are handled both before and after our deaths, we must educate ourselves about what trusts are and how they differ from wills. Wills used to be the vehicle of choice because trusts were regarded as solely instruments of the wealthy allowing them to lock up fortunes for generations. Even people with vast amounts of wealth had wills—they still do—but wills seemed to be open to greedy heirs and fortune hunters who wanted to get a piece of the pie.

Trusts seemed to be an ironclad vehicle that could not be broken by anyone. It was a secret way of preserving assets by placing them out of the reach of naïve children and under the control of prudent, business-savvy trustees. Both scenarios, however, were and still are, in large part, a myth. Both wills and trusts are subject to all kinds of abuse and fraud. I once handled a case of a wealthy heiress whose will was a mess. The estate took over fifteen years to settle. The assets consisted of raw land, leases, a closely held corporation, securities, options, a residence, several residential buildings, an office building, property in other states, art work, jewelry, etc. valued at over $112 million. Despite the fact that legions of lawyers had prepared the estate documents, no plan had been devised for dealing with the estate administration. The land value pushed the estate into a high tax bracket but the land was not owned outright by the estate so could not be sold to meet this liability. Thirty-two named beneficiaries located all over the world had their own ideas how to administer the estate and meet their individual needs and demands. The IRS also had its own demands for estate tax.

In the end administrative costs and attorney fees took close to $8 million. The court and experts took close to half a million. Had the grantor anticipated events relating to her estate she could have avoided at least half this cost. She had left the planning up to a legion of lawyers who drafted her will, but they missed accounting for the most important event that occurred—her dying without children—and her estate suffered greatly because of it. In short, there are many different ways you can handle your estate, and all are open to negligence, mistakes, abuse, and fraud if you do not plan properly.

Four Methods for Disposing of Our Wealth:

While there are a myriad of ways to acquire wealth there are really only four methods for disposing of it. We can:

- do nothing and let the government dispose of it for us;
- give it away to charity;
- contract it away through a will; or
- place it in a trust.

Perhaps because we have not had wealth issues to deal with, our estate plan has often suffered from little or last-minute attention. We hastily write a will, stick it in a drawer and move on. We don't like to think about our own demise, so it is an area ripe for abuse. If we do not think about it or plan for it and rely on someone else to make the decisions for us, how can we expect it to turn out the way we want? It is like designing a house but omitting the detail of how it is to be built.

Even though many of you have already gone through the estate-planning process, few of you are probably aware of the ways in which your wealth could be distributed and disposed of after you die. The four possible scenarios listed above provide different risks and benefits:

Intestate Estate: If you do nothing, then the law steps in and writes a will or trust for you. This is called "intestate estate" and it is the worst scenario for anyone. If you die without a trust or will, the law appoints an estate administrator and takes out of your estate all the relative court costs and probate fees, taxes, court administration fees, appraisals, inventory experts, lawyers, accountants, and tax preparers fees. If there is anything left after this process, the law divides your estate according to applicable state law among your legal heirs, who may or may not be the people you wanted to receive your assets.

Giving Money to Charities: You have the option of giving your assets away in whole or in part to charities. There may be certain tax advantages for your estate if charitable giving is combined with the estate plan. While many people willingly choose to let all or part of their estate go to charities, if you choose this route, know that, like trusts, you must do your homework because the funds often never reach the intended charitable beneficiary. Assuring that your funds actually accomplish the purpose for which the gift was made in the first place depends on how well the gift was planned, what safeguards you put in place for its administration, and how reliable the person(s) you placed in charge are. Whether your directives are followed has always been based on trusting the person you appoint. Just as money and assets can be siphoned off of your estate for purposes other than the gift, charities are sometimes guilty of the same problems. While there are a number of issues that you must be aware of when you give all or part of your estate to charities, I am not going to delve into them here. If you want to find out more about charitable giving, please visit www.suefarley.com.

The Difference between a Will and a Trust

In many old movies, from murder mysteries to comedies, one of the opening scenes is often a group of money-hungry heirs sitting around a lawyer's conference table eagerly waiting to hear the will read. It had all sorts of conflicts waiting to erupt, greed and family strife the most common. Wills certainly have a place in estate planning, and I intend to help educate you more thoroughly about them in my next book and on my company website fiduciarytechnologiesinc.com, which will focus on the estate and trust administrative process. For now, what you need to know is that there's not a huge difference between a will and a trust. Having said that, if you know how to administer a will, you know how to administer a trust. All of the early procedures of a will are similar for a trust. However, because the trust lasts for so much longer, there's more planning involved with it than with a will. Oh, and one bit of advice I will give you now: when you write your trust documents, you should also have what is called a Pour Over Will. This is a will that takes care of all the assets you have not placed in trust. It directs that any assets you hold at death that are not part of your trust are to be transferred on death into your trust. Definitely discuss this type of will with your estate planner.

Definitions

The "will" is a legally binding written document that directs the disposition of assets after death and names the legal representative, the "executor," who will administer the estate of the decedent. The will itself and how property is viewed and handled by the law in an estate is the product of hundreds of years of legal evolution, but the main difference between a will and a trust is that a will is handled by the Probate Court who oversees the handling of the estate. "Probate" is the legal process related to the administration of the estate of a decedent who created a will. The named executor files the decedent's will with the probate court, submits an inventory of the decedent's property along with appraisals of the estates asset value, pays the legal debts and taxes, and distributes the remaining assets and property to the beneficiaries or heirs of the estate. If the will is in good order and all the named beneficiaries in the will can be found, the estate is handled usually within one to two years.

Trusts, however, have become main stream. They are the estate planner's preferred planning tool. In 2001, the Internal Revenue Service (IRS) reported 3.92 million fiduciary tax returns were filed, up from 1.7 million in 1976. By 2009, the IRS projects the number of fiduciary tax returns filed to increase to 4.25 million. And these numbers do not include the number of "revocable trusts," or "living trusts" that currently hold a huge amount of wealth but do not report the wealth on a separate fiduciary return.

As I said in the introduction, a "trust" is a legal document giving control of the grantor's property to another person or entity called a "trustee." The trustee holds title to the assets and operates in the place of the grantor for the benefit of the "beneficiary" of the trust.

There are a number of different types of trusts, but they generally fall into two categories: complex or simple. Simple trusts are more like wills in that they distribute out after the person dies; the trust stays in effect only as long as it takes to distribute the assets. The IRS defines it by three main conditions:

- income cannot go to charitable beneficiaries;
- distributions may not be made from the corpus of the trust (property of the trust);
- all income has to be distributed to the beneficiaries of the trust and on termination all assets are distributed to the named beneficiaries.
- Once the assets are distributed, the trust is terminated.

The complex trusts are the type we're more familiar with—the ones that distribute assets over a long period of time, two generations or more, into the future. A complex trust can make distributions to charities, distribute amounts from the property of the trust, retain some of the current income of the trust under the trust's terms, and last for a very long time.

There are two subcategories to the complex trust. The first category is the "*irrevocable trust.*" It is generally a complex trust, and it is a written document creating a separate legal entity that directs the administration of assets placed in the trust. It cannot be revoked or terminated except by its own terms or by court order. This type of trust can be created two ways. The grantor can create an irrevocable trust during his or her lifetime, whereby property is transferred irrevocably to a separate legal entity, the trust, under the control and direction of the trustee. In an irrevocable trust the grantor gives up ownership and control of the assets placed in trust. He/she transfers absolute power and control over these assets to the person designated as trustee. The grantor cannot later change his mind and undo the trust or recover the assets.

The irrevocable trust can also be set up at the time of the grantor's death in something called a "testamentary trust." This type of trust is created by a will and springs to life when the grantor dies. It is usually subject to continuing court supervision. With the testamentary trust, the court operates in a manner similar to a probate court to oversee the trust's administration.

The second subcategory of trust is the "*revocable trust*" more commonly referred to as a "*living trust*" and what the IRS calls a "*grantor trust.*" It is created during the lifetime of the grantor where the grantor transfers title and ownership of his/her assets to the trust but the grantor serves as the trust's first trustee, thus retaining control over the property until he/she dies. As trustee he/she controls the disposition of assets during his/her lifetime, is treated as the owner of the trust, and names a successor trustee to distribute the assets at death

The revocable trust is a simple trust because it pays out on death to the beneficiaries. It is different from the irrevocable trust in that it can be terminated by the grantor as long as the grantor is alive. This trust becomes irrevocable on the death of the grantor. It allows the creation of a trust similar to a will for the purpose of the estate avoiding probate.

> **Trust Tip**
>
> A "living trust" should not be confused with a "living will." The "living will" is only used to deal with life and death directives. It tells your family and your doctors what you want to have happen in case you find yourself in a situation where you are alive but unable to speak for yourself. If you want to find out more about living wills, or want to make your own, please visit www.suefarley. com and download your free report.

One of the important benefits of a "living" or "grantor" trust is that it allows us to plan for our own care while we are alive because it transitions our assets to the trustee of our estate when we are no longer able to care for ourselves. One of the hardest facts to confront as we create a trust like this is that, as we age, our perspective may be skewed by different brain activity, depression, Alzheimer's, or the onset of dementia. It is important that we plan for this eventuality. The living trust is essential in this respect as it can be designed so that even our care is transitioned to our designated trustee. Ideally the trustee will handle matters consistent with our directives.

There is a third type of trust that is gaining in popularity. It is a type of irrevocable trust is called the "*perpetual trust,*" and is sometimes known as the "*Dynasty Trust.*" These are trusts that people use as a way to avoid estate taxes entirely. This type of trust is one that can last forever or almost forever depending on which state you adopt as the home base for the trust. And while the dynasty trust can keep your assets out of the hands of the government, you must know that in the long term, your beneficiaries may not be protected because the administrators can hold the assets forever and pay themselves forever for doing so. I always tell people, if you have millions to lose, and you want to avoid estate taxes, by all means, look into a dynasty trust. However, in my opinion, I think these trusts are a sucker's bet, because the beneficiaries may see only a small amount of the assets of the trust since the administrator can always limit distributions on the excuse that they have to plan and preserve assets for an indefinite number of future generations. The trustee gets fees based on assets under management so it is in the trustee's interest to limit distributions. Obviously, I do not promote these types of trusts, and I only mention them here. If you want to know more about the perpetual trust, please go to suefarley. com where I discuss in dept why I think these trusts are a bad idea.

Most important, remember there can be tax complications with any trust, so as always make sure you talk to your tax expert about all of your options before you commit to any one.

Traditional Estate Planning

Pros and Cons of Wills: When people think of estate planning, they think of lawyers, expense, and hours of work creating the information necessary for putting an estate plan together. As I noted earlier, because the process is stressful and uncomfortable, we usually want to terminate it as quickly as possible. We rely on our lawyer to choose the legal format, calculate our tax exposure, and give us their expert analysis of which form(s) will best fill our goals, wishes, and directives. We sign the papers in front of a notary and are finished. The document goes into the safe or a drawer and we breathe a sigh of relief that we are finished. If we had to explain why we chose a will or a trust, we would repeat what our lawyer told us, but we probably don't know the difference.

But giving up your responsibility for understanding the difference and knowing which type of estate-planning instrument is best for you is unwise. If you do not understand the document that has been prepared for you, how do you know that it will play out as you expect? A   will by definition is a "testamentary instrument" since it becomes effective only when you die, you never know whether it worked or not.

As I defined above, the will carries with it a whole legal process called "probate" that is a formal court proceeding to assure that the debts are paid and assets distributed according to the terms of the will and according to the forms, procedures, time frame and directives of the court. One might think from this brief description that the process is relatively simple; it is not. While some estates are more complicated than others, suffice it to say I've handled estates that have taken many years to close. This does not mean that if it had been a simple trust it would have closed any sooner. It just means that the issues we do not resolve before our deaths will consume a large portion of our assets when we are gone.

For all the negative things that are said and written about probate— it is expensive and bureaucratic—the positive aspect of a will and its accompanying probate is that there is a process set forth that defines the procedures necessary to terminate the interest of the deceased, pay the debts, and distribute the assets. Because it is supervised by the court, accountings must be done, values must be established, taxes paid, businesses closed, and assets sold in a relatively formal order. If things are not moving as they should, the court can intercede to assure that it will be done correctly. Additionally those who object are flushed out and rulings made either for or against them and there is finality to the proceeding at its end.

The downside of a will is that it involves lawyers, court proceedings, formal procedures, formal valuations of assets, probate referees, open disclosure in a public forum, a time frame often governed by the courts and lawyers—all of which are very costly. Though many are surprised at probate's extensive procedures and requirements, a properly administered trust borrows most of these same procedures but on an informal basis.

Pro's and Con's of Trusts: The benefits of a trust generally are that they can be created while we are alive, managed under our supervision (if it is a revocable trust), and continue in effect at our death without the necessity of formal court proceedings. The cost of probate is avoided, upfront costs are minimized, and assets are preserved to the family. While avoiding taxes *per se* should not be the sole purpose for creating a trust, trusts can be used as a vehicle for minimizing estate taxes and thus maximize the benefits to the beneficiaries. Trusts are also private—family issues and fortunes are not aired in the public forum of a probate court. The probate court will only become involved when there are disputes.

The problems with trusts generally include what's called the "broad grant of authority" to the trustee over assets. This means your trustee can do whatever he or she pleases with your assets. Some trustees work very hard in the name of their trust; however, some trustees act in their own interests and claim it is for the benefit of the trust. The problem comes from the fact the trust is not supervised by anyone. Procedures for reporting, maintaining records, or being responsive to the needs of the beneficiaries are subject to the trustee's discretion. Despite the legal requirements imposed on the trustee, there is no ready enforcement mechanism other than filing a lawsuit against the trustee to enforce the trust's provisions. The trustee may be a family member or other person with no training in trust administration, and there are no readily accessible defined procedures and processes guiding him or her through the administrative process. As a result every trustee does it his/her own way, which may or may not comply with applicable laws.

Contrary to popular belief, you do not totally avoid probate by creating a trust. Most of the steps in administering a trust should be done in a manner consistent with your state's applicable probate laws. While the administrative procedures for a trust are less formal, so are the safeguards. The trustee is left to self-validate his/her own administrative process and decisions, and this leaves the door open for problems and abuse. The beneficiaries can seek to have the trust enforced through a court proceeding, but in reality the beneficiaries are usually dependent upon the trust for support and can ill afford to alienate the person upon whom they depend for support. Similarly the beneficiaries usually do not have an independent source of funds to pay for a court challenge to the trustee's conduct. Also, as I noted in the introduction, the trustee can take funds from the trust to defend against the attack.

The Goal of the Will versus the Trust

Your decision between a will and a trust depends upon what you want to accomplish. This will involve some self-examination about what you want for your heirs and an examination of the assets you have. Each estate-planning instrument has specific goals attached to them, as outlined here:

The Goal of a Will: The goal of the administration of a will is to pay the debts and distribute the estate as soon as feasibly possible. It must be understood that a will by its nature cannot be prolonged for any purpose but to resolve issues which stand in the way of distribution of assets. Any provision that carries with it contingent directives such as, "I give $10,000.00 to my nephew if he goes to college," and the nephew is six years old when the gift is granted, will not keep the estate open waiting for the decision of the minor to go to college. The court will simply place the funds in trust for the child with the parent as trustee or distribute it to the parents as guardian for the child. In order to meet the goal of a will—the clean distribution of your estate—you must provide a way to untangle your affairs so anyone can step in on your death and resolve the issues quickly.

The Goal of a Trust: Because a trust distributes trust assets over time, it generally has more complex goals than a will. First, a trust should have a "material purpose"; in other words it must be shown that the creator of the trust has a "particular concern or objective" which prompted the creation of the trust in the first place. The National Conference of Commissioners on Uniform State Laws notes that "There should be evidence that the trust arrangement represented to the Settlor [another term for "grantor"] more than a method of allocating the benefits of property among multiple beneficiaries or a means of offering to the beneficiaries (but not imposing on them) a particular advantage." In short the "material purpose" of the trust is dependent upon all the facts and circumstances surrounding its creation. Why was the trust created? If the purpose is tax avoidance, this may be an insufficient reason to prolong the trust beyond the period of tax saving. So too, showing a particular concern by the grantor for a beneficiary's management skills, judgment, or level of maturity may be insufficient to prolong the trust beyond educating the beneficiary and their demonstration of working and management skills.

In some states where no "purpose" or "goal" of the trust is set forth, or the purpose has been completed, the trust can be terminated. There is a movement across the country to adopt uniform laws to this effect. The National Conference of Commissioners on Uniform State Laws has instituted rules governing the termination of trusts. Under the Revised Uniform Trust Code an irrevocable non-charitable trust can be terminated early "if no purpose of the trust remains to be achieved or the purposes of the trust have become unlawful, contrary to public policy, or impossible to achieve." Where all beneficiaries consent, the trust may also be terminated where there is no material purpose to the trust.

Since a trust can last for decades, time should be spent defining goals and establishing parameters for decision making. Determine whether the goal can reasonably be accomplished during the life of the trust. Has the stage been set so there is funding? Are the people you named as trustees willing to dedicate time and energy to accomplishing the trust's goals, and complying with performance standards? In one case I know of, even when the charitable trust accomplished its goal of funding the construction of a wing on a museum, the administrators of the trust decided to interpret the goal of "construction" not to be the sole purpose of the trust. Since the language was ambiguous, the administration continued for as long as there were funds to pay the administrators benefiting no one else but the administrators!

Who's in Charge?

Both wills and trusts have entities that oversee their execution. In its simplest terms, a will has an executor and a trust has a trustee.

The role of the personal representative whether they serve as trustee or executor will be similar. Yet there are a few differences that should be understood up front.

The Will: Under a will your executor is the person who oversees the whole probate process. Usually you can name anyone who is competent and an adult (over eighteen) to serve in this capacity. People often name their lawyers, but any adult can be named to fill the role.

The job of the executor is to settle the estate and distribute the assets. The estate is usually subject to court supervision, so there are demands made upon the executor for reporting, meeting deadlines, assembling inventories, appraisements, meeting with court representatives, dealing with the IRS, meeting tax obligations within short deadlines, managing and preserving the assets, dealing with creditors and lawyers and dealing with family. This relatively demanding job can consume hundreds of hours depending upon the complexity of the estate. Who you choose should understand the role they are to play and the requirements of the job.

It is important to contemplate whether your executor has the staying power to perform the tasks required. Family members generally want to do a good job but because they lack training, accountings, deadlines, and reporting requirements often suffer from their naïveté. As the years pass and the requirements of the job are not met, monetary losses begin to occur without much notice. They are only caught when the personal representative is forced to account and report, and the discovery of the lost money then erupts into family disputes and worse litigation.

Who you choose to represent you in the probating of your will can have a profound impact on what your beneficiaries receive. If it is done right the probate process should preserve the assets for the ultimate beneficiaries. The fees proscribed for the executor are usually based on the value of the estate and defined in the state probate code, but they are always conditioned upon the fiduciary performing his/her job. Costs can skyrocket when the executor retains lawyers, accountants, appraisers, property managers, auctioneers, tax attorneys, etc.

While your assets are under the control of your executor, the beneficiaries receive limited information about what is sold and retained by the executor, and they have little input into the process except through formal court proceedings. What is left after this process may be smaller than anticipated.

The simple truth is, the more organized you are before you die, the more current your estate documents, the clearer your directives, the less the cost of probating your estate. For example, if you prepare your own inventory of your belongings and make sure to attach relative values to each item, your personal representative can use it and avoid the time and expense of compiling this information from scratch. If you can, provide a brief history of yourself and your heirs including birth dates, marriage dates, second marriage history, and step children history and contact information; it will provide your trustee with an understanding of who your heirs are as well as allow them to participate in the administrative process. In order to have your will play out as you wish, you must provide letters of instruction directing your executor regarding your burial wishes and the sale of assets to meet anticipated taxes. The letter of instructions should also deal with issues with respect to difficult assets like closely held corporations, foreign assets, real property, and specialty items like art, jewelry, etc. All this work will preserve the assets for your beneficiaries.

The Trust: The personal representative we name as our trustee steps into our shoes and acts on our behalf. The role of trustee differs from the executor in one simple aspect: the trustee is to act on our behalf, trying to handle the estate according to our wishes, whereas the executor acts only to close the estate. Trustees can, like executors, be anyone who is over eighteen years of age and is competent. Usually the trustee is either a professional fiduciary, a personal trustee, a family member or friend.

The role of trustee, unlike the executor, extends beyond death sometimes indefinitely into the future. Unless court supervision is required by the trust instrument, the trustee will serve with no independent supervision. The trust administrator can also serve in the role of both executor and trustee if so named by the grantor. Once the trustee is appointed he/she immediately becomes responsible for the assets of the trust, for filing tax returns, securing and managing the assets, determining the goal of the trust and mapping a course to accomplish it all. So too the trustee is responsible for accounting and reporting to the beneficiaries, and addressing all the issues outlined in the trust instrument. What is often forgotten is that the trustee serves for life or for however long the trust lasts. Once appointed, it is difficult and costly to remove a trustee. Trusts as they are currently written have neglect, inattention and mismanagement built into the them because typically the trustee has direction for about 25 percent of the tasks he/she is expected to perform.

With a lifetime appointment and no supervision of the trust, the trustee can operate with little to no oversight from others. One major disadvantage of a personal trustee is that self-validation is usually a trap for the inexperienced trustee. He or she begins to believe that his/her decisions and conduct are above challenge and that the assets are his/hers to do with as he/she chooses. In this regard, the design of the trust often fails because there are no checks and balances provided to assure that the goals of the trust are reached, and there are no processes or procedures for catching the errant trustee in the improper use of trust assets.

In addition, the trustee has no safeguards to protect him or her from challenge by the beneficiary since formal court approval has been eliminated. This means that the trustee carries the liability for his or her actions over the course of the administrative process. There is no real finality or relief from liability for the trustee except as provided in the trust instrument or by the statute of limitations (a legal period within which the beneficiaries must file a lawsuit to redress a wrong). The beneficiaries can second-guess the actions of the trustee sometimes many years after the challenged action, and the trustee suffers as a result. Any loss suffered by the trust by reason of the proven negligence, mismanagement, or fraud of the trustee has to be paid back to the trust by the trustee out of his/her/its personal assets. So when you're asking a person to be your personal representative, you need to let them know that by doing so, he or she has placed his personal assets at risk for replenishing the trust for his or her administrative mistakes.

Despite all of these problems, the trust remains, in most instances, the best vehicle for estate planning simply because it provides the most flexibility for dealing with assets and beneficiaries. Because it is often the best option, we need to look at all the different aspects that go into the making of a trust so that we can ensure that the trusts we create function better, are more accountable, and protect our assets from loss.

CHAPTER TWO

Creating the Road Map of Your Trust: The Main Ingredients

Ultimately, the purpose of this book is to tell you about the problems that are rife within most estate plans and offer you some solutions on how to fix them. Even though you now have a broad overview of trusts and what they're supposed to do, I want to do a little bit more to educate you on all the elements that go into an estate plan. It's not just about taxes, even though that's what your estate planner is going to focus on. There are facets of a trust that work well in the current system, but one of the problems with a trust is that most people don't want to actually sit down and do it. When I ask people if they currently have a will or a trust they usually respond either, "Yes, but it needs to be updated," or "No, I have to do one." No one wants to sit down and confront planning their trust for a number of reasons.

First, writing a trust makes a person confront their skeletons. Some are scarier than others, like what to do with the illegitimate child that you've never taken responsibility for or the son that you haven't spoken to in thirty years (both scenarios I've had to deal with, by the way). Sometimes, it's that you have to face up to preferential treatment of one child over the other, even when it's legitimate. What do you do, for example, with your daughter who is living with a drug dealer or is an alcoholic? Do you give that child the same share as the other kids?

I've also had people tell me they were reluctant to finalize their trusts because they want to remain in control of their money forever. They want to set up a dynasty trust because it was a way to extend their hand from the grave, so to speak. If they have their money tied up in trust, they essentially get to dictate how that money is going to be distributed because the trustee remains in control of the money as long as there is money to be controlled. That is certainly your choice, but know that if you do that you're not benefiting the only people you care about and know best in this world—your spouse, your children, and perhaps your grandchildren. The rest of your family who would be benefiting from the trust are really just future-generations you know nothing about, and to these future generations, you're just a name thrown about with maybe a picture on a wall to commemorate your generosity.

Now if you have billions of dollars, like say the Rockefellers, then by all means do something that does impact future generations. But instead of giving money to people, I suggest setting up a trust that builds a museum or a library. Do things that will be a legacy of good that transcends generations and that will benefit mankind. So the first point I want to make about planning your trust is to give your assets to those immediately around you, your spouse, kids and/or grandkids, and leave it at that. The hard fact is, when you're gone, you can't control what happens to your money and much of it will be siphoned off by third parties just to administer your trust.

My Own Experience

How do I know how difficult it is to write a trust? Because I recently had to deal with writing my own. Even with all of my experience, I had never gone through the process; I knew what I was in for, so I just kept putting it off. I didn't do it until I was forced to. I had to undergo spine surgery that could leave me dead or a paraplegic. I was hoping for the opposite, but I had to face the facts nonetheless. It occurred to me that I had no time between when I realized I had to write the trust and the date of surgery to undertake the onerous process of finding an estate planner and undertaking the gruesome task of writing a trust or a will. "Well," I thought, "I am a lawyer specializing in estate and trust administration and I have seen the horrors of the estate and trust plans that did not work."

At this point, I had started my company that was putting together a technological architecture for estate planners and administrators to link their trusts and wills to an administrative plan. I knew more than most about the process, so I decided to do it myself. After all any written document that is signed, dated, and witnessed by two witnesses can be a legitimate will or trust in my state and many others. I would simply draft it in a manner consistent with all state laws so there would be no issue with its legitimacy.

I am quite aware of the reality that we suffer from the same wishful thinking that all we have to do is write down what we want before we die and there will be people who will step forward to accomplish exactly what we want, how we want it, and when we want it done. I'm aware that relying on others to do as I ask after I'm gone is not a sure thing. While there are family members who love us dearly and want to do the right thing, lots of problems emerge at our death that we do not anticipate. But I was amazed at how quickly these issues surfaced as I worked through setting up my trust. For example, I found that the "right thing" to my husband did not mean the same "right thing" to my daughter, his stepdaughter. I also discovered that my daughter and son did not always agree on how decisions are made, and they definitely disagreed on how best to deal with me, my assets, or for that matter how to deal with my husband, their stepfather, and vice versa.

I have to admit, even knowing all that I know about what makes a good estate plan, I was shocked at how hard it was to deal with some pretty heavy issues which we would rather ignore. Yet they are important issues that deserve our attention not only for our own peace of mind but for the peace of mind of those we love. If we fail to address these issues, we leave ourselves and our families at risk—subject to the default provisions of the law that apply when we have failed to address the issues for ourselves. I knew the repercussions of my leaving important decisions up to someone else, and I for one would rather be making decisions for myself and my family rather than leaving them to the courts and third parties.

While we may have a loving family with the best of intentions, it is important that we create a clear road map for those who follow us so we can guide them as to our wishes, goals, and desires with respect to our assets and family care. To leave them in the dark with broad discretion to do as they think best grants too much power to family members and often results in resentment and family division. Often the views shared by your named trustee are not the views shared by the rest of the family. Knowing this, I attempted to avoid family tensions by making the directives in my trust specific. I know that at this stage of the game, while I'm still alive, it is I, not they, who should be making the decisions. I knew the importance of addressing the issues that I could foresee and taking the time to contemplate the contingent events that could occur in my family or in society that could thwart my own goals and desires. I conscientiously planned for them by anticipating them and then addressing them in my trust.

Many of the issues I had to face aren't any different from issues most people face. First, I had to deal with the immediate tax liability of my estate. I had to figure out what assets I wanted sold to meet this liability as well as provide directions as to how I wanted my home, animals, company, retirement plan, stocks, bonds, furniture, business, jewelry, etc. taken care of. Some key questions I had to answer are: Do I want my representative to account to my heirs? Do I expect honesty and integrity from those who represent me? Do I want my trust to be transparent—meaning that everything is as clearly defined as possible—to those who benefit so they can monitor the person placed in charge? Do I want to empower my beneficiaries to get rid of an untrustworthy representative? How long do I want to tie up my assets? What benefit(s) do I want to grant to my heirs and when?

As one might expect, this was an emotional roller coaster. It could not be done in one day or one week. It spanned months while I analyzed options, talked to people who said they would help, and evaluated the best and worst qualities of the individuals who I contemplated naming as my beneficiaries and representatives. I tried to think of the worst scenario and plan for it. I tried to eliminate obstacles to full distribution like taxes, appraisals, sales at auctions, family squabbles, etc.

I decided that the best estate plan for me was a simple trust. I'm not interested in tying up my assets. I wanted to get them to my husband and to my children as soon as they were able to handle them. I chose this because I feel strongly that if my children make mistakes, then so be it. It is better that they make mistakes with the money than have the funds tied up and being managed by someone else. That would put my assets at risk of being lost or taken by third parties. My children have been raised to look out for themselves with a view that they must be self-supporting after college and grad school. They know they have to earn money to survive. I have instilled in them the importance of an education, and I trust and believe in their judgment.

I was also well aware at the time I drew up my trust that if I died, I would never know whether all my planning worked out the way that I wanted it to. But I took solace in something I've seen happen time and again: when you believe in someone, they often have the odd reaction of trying to justify that belief. I am actually counting on this with my children. I knew that they would grow up quickly in my absence because their father had already died and the loss of both parents can be devastating. I put in place as many advisors as I could muster to help them (my husband, my brother, their father's brother and sisters, and friends). But I didn't make these people actual trustees; I left the decision up to my kids as to whether they want to tap into these resources. I also have a mother requiring attention and she needed to be provided for. I also made sure that I was clear about what I wanted for my second husband. He had a previous family with two children, and I made sure to reference our prenuptial agreement that provides that assets belonging to us before marriage are our separate property.

In the end, I think I made a pretty clear map of what I wanted my trust to do. I divided my assets as simply as I could. I divided my property that is separate from my husband's equally between my two children in a living trust. I have a pre-marital life insurance policy that provides benefits to my mother to care for her until she dies and then those assets go to my children. My brother is requested to care for my mother. My community property is divided between my husband and my children. I made specific gifts and wrote checks to each of my two children within the gift limit ($12,000 per year right now; I'll go into gift limits in a moment) so the funds would not pass through my estate. I then wrote personal letters to each of my children, my mom, and husband saying goodbye. While I survived the operation quite fine, suffice it to say I would not want to go through this again real soon. But I know it won't be as hard the next time because I have already "been there and done that." I also know that I will have to revisit the trust as my husband and I grow older, acquire more assets, and prepare for our retirement years.

Creating an Estate Plan—The Big Picture

I told you my story to get you thinking about the kinds of decisions you will need to make if you don't have a trust or will or need to update your existing one. As I hinted at the end of my story, the estate planning process should not be a one-time event. The plan we create today with a snapshot of our family, our assets, and our goals and wishes changes with time. The law, personal relationships, and events that occur and change our lives warrant changes in our estate plan. Because we now have to deal with an increased amount of wealth, we need to understand the dynamics of estate planning and use it as a hedge against unforeseen events. We *must* provide a map for our heirs so our affairs may be adequately attended to by our personal representative when we're no longer able to do so ourselves.

When to Begin an Estate Plan

As you start contemplating how you want your map to look, you need to first decide where you are now. In terms of estate planning, that means your age. I've been asked countless times, "I'm still young and healthy, so when should I begin my estate plan?" Traditionally estate planning began at age fifty or older. In earlier times, estate planning was left until the time of death because no one wanted to deal with it and there was generally little to pass on. Fortunately, the baby-boom generation recognizes the importance of estate planning because they are seeing their aging parents who have either failed to address estate issues, leaving them to deal with the clean up, or their parents have planned their estates well and are reaping the benefits.

But how does one plan an estate well? There is growing recognition by young people ages twenty-five and up who may have been beneficiaries of a trust or received an inheritance from their grandparents that they too need to know more about the estate planning and administrative process. Many are being asked by family members to serve as trustees of their parent's trusts or to take care of ailing or disabled family members. Yet despite a willingness to serve, few have any training in this area or know what to do. Information in this area is difficult to obtain because it is designed mostly for the lawyer, but it is the family member, not the lawyer, who is likely to be appointed as the successor trustee to their parent or sibling because it seems fitting to name a family member who knows their family, assets, and issues better. Also we have grown to distrust the professional because of the stories we have heard from disgruntled beneficiaries or because we do not want to endure the formality or incur professional fees.

Most important, planning an estate should commence early and be revisited often. If you are setting up a plan for the first time, it may be a simple plan, but that's okay because the planning will evolve over time. Also I have found, it helps to think of estate planning not as "death planning"—what many like to call it—but as a living financial-planning tool for your family that evolves as your life changes. Whether your estate plan was created a year prior to your death or ten years prior may have significant consequences on whether your heirs receive their inheritance. Time, life events, undisclosed facts, and new circumstances can have a dramatic impact on an estate plan. The picture you had of how life would play out when you created the plan can change overnight. It can also gradually change over time as the people you rely on become less reliable by reason of their own changed circumstances or the simple aging process. Jobs, relationships, assets, and family have a way of evolving to different stages often in a way that was not anticipated. For these reasons the estate plan should not be stagnant but a living financial-planning tool. *It should be updated every three years* or at the time of a trigger event.

Five Events That Trigger Planning Requirements

There are five basic "trigger events" that prompt a person to begin the estate-planning process:

1. The birth of a child: When a child is born, we think about life, but like it or not, we need to institute a plan to take care of the child if we die or are incapacitated. Unless you plan to give the child to adoptive authorities, the child's birth must trigger estate planning. Who will take care of the child? Who will pay for its support, education, and welfare? If something were to happen to you, whom would you want in charge of the child? How would you like the child raised? Have you conveyed to anyone what you want for your child? Do you have life insurance for the child? Each parent is responsible for the health, education, and welfare of each child they bring into this world, and you need to plan for the unexpected.

2. *Accumulated Assets of $250K or more:* As young adults, we are often so caught up accumulating and creating wealth that we ignore our own success and fail to address certain stages of life that require our attention. The generation of wealth carries with it a responsibility to take care of it and to plan for it. A recent study at a major business school found that 65 percent of those studied, regardless of their own net worth, felt the need to start planning a trust or will when their net worth approached $250K.

3. *Marriage:* Marriage tends to be a life trigger for a lot of things, and one of those things should be estate planning. Estate planning begins to address those assets that are owned separately by us before our marriage as well as assets accumulated as a couple. How and what do you want to provide for your spouse and others? Even if you have a prenuptial agreement, the estate plan directs your representative about its existence and direction.

a. *Out-of-Marriage Relationships:* If you are living together or have a life partner, planning is even more important since the state intestate laws (laws that apply to people who have no plan) often do not treat these relationships in the same manner as marriage. Thus it is important to set out what you want, whose property belongs to whom, and what rights to jointly acquired property you want to assert. If you have a relationship with another human being, one that you cherish or despise, your wishes will be ignored unless they are properly set out in a plan. Do not leave your partner in the dark.

4. *Buying a House:* As a major asset, buying a home usually represents a significant commitment of funds and responsibility. Because of their appreciation in value, you need to set out a plan to deal with its maintenance, debt servicing, and disposition (how you want to dispose of it) if you die or are incapacitated. In fact the acquisition of any real estate triggers the obligation to plan for it in the event of your own death.

5. Reaching Age Thirty to Forty: By the time you are thirty and moving on to age forty, you probably have at least started and are hopefully well into figuring out who you are and what you are doing with your life. By this time you have had sufficient time to accumulate assets and should also be planning for them so that what you have worked for does not simply pass by default to the IRS or relatives.

Estate Taxes and Government Benefits[2]

There are obviously many areas that you need to address as you map out your estate plan. However, before we get into the more ill-defined areas of the planning process, I'm going to address the one issue that everyone will face—taxes. The biggest myth about trusts is that they are generally thought of as tax shelters, but because taxes are usually on the forefront of most peoples' minds, I'm going to give you some of the basics here. This does not mean that I'm going to go in-depth. I've included at www.suefarley.com a report that tells you about the various kinds of trusts and the tax benefits of each. I suggest that you study it, after you read this book and before you go to an estate planner, so you will be more able to talk about what you need and want with your estate planner.

However, I must start this section with a disclaimer. Taxes in general require an expertise and discussion that is beyond this book. The ins and outs of tax planning *must* be discussed with a tax expert. While the primary purpose of a will or trust is to pass on your assets and your values in a manner you control, tax and benefit planning should not be overlooked. Depending on your personal/family situation, different trust mechanisms can have a big impact on the amount and timing of the taxes or the benefits the beneficiaries will ultimately receive. This section will provide you with an overview of the most commonly used estate mechanisms and discuss the language used and mechanisms employed.

---

2   Peter Meyer Esq. of Oakland a talented estate planner helped with the review of this section and the appendix as I am not a tax lawyer.

Taxes Generally

The first thing you must know is that trusts in and of themselves are not tax-avoidance mechanisms. Even if you have a simple trust, estate taxes still must be paid at death if your estate's value is large enough to be taxable. Trusts are attractive because you have the power to take certain assets out of your estate, place them in trust, and reduce estate taxes. Assets transferred permanently out of your name and placed into a trust over which you relinquish complete control will not be taxed as part of your estate. However, simply transferring assets out of your name may not keep the IRS from taking a share. Unfortunately, if your wealth is above certain limits, the largest amount of taxes you may ever have to pay occurs when you die in the form of estate taxes (what some deridingly call the "death tax"). Most people think of taxes as tax on income. But in an estate the tax is not on income. Estate and gift taxes are based on the "market value" of all assets held on the date of death. Estate tax is paid out of your estate and is due nine months after you die. Whether you have provided enough in liquid assets (assets that can be converted to cash quickly) to meet this liability within the specified deadline for the payment will depend upon how well you have planned. If you have not planned how your estate will meet this tax liability, then your heirs will be faced with selling off your personal property, real property, and other assets in a rush to meet the tax deadline. This type of "fire sale" often results in significant loss to the estate. So too it may result in liquidating the most available assets whether they should have been preserved or not.

If you think, "Ah ha I will just give my money away before I die and I will avoid the estate tax," think again. This would be a good plan, but the government has already thought of this and hits you with a gift tax. I don't think it's coincidence that the gift tax (with some exceptions) is taxed at the same rate as the estate tax; the government gets its share no matter what. Both estate and gift taxes can be higher than your personal income tax. In 2010, it will be 45 percent, but in the past it reached 60 percent or more depending upon the amount of the gift or estate. (Giving assets to a charity, however, does not usually carry the gift tax or estate tax problems and can be beneficial to your planning). If there is one thing that I have learned about taxes, trust the professionals. It is not an area for dabbling. The landscape is an ever-changing one, and you need current tax advice on the situation that confronts you.

But since my purpose is to educate you, I will give you an overall picture of how estate and gift taxes work. The government calculates your estate tax based on the fair market value of assets held by you at death. The gift tax is based on the cumulative value of current and prior gifts. Every brokerage account, parcel of real estate, insurance policy, retirement account, tangible personal property and other asset you own at death that is not transferred out of your name gets calculated into the gross value of your estate—the larger the estate, the larger the tax.

The chart I've given you here sets forth the way the IRS calculates your estate or gift tax right now in 2008. I specify "right now" because the IRS is always issuing regulations, new revenue rulings, and other changes to the tax code. The top estate and gift tax rate remains at 45 percent through 2009.

Value or Estate or Gift Exceeding $	Up to	Taxed at %
$0	$12,000	0%
$12,000	20,000	20%
20,000	40,000	22%
40,000	60,000	24%
60,000	80,000	26%
80,000	100,000	28%
100,000	150,000	30%
150,000	250,000	32%
250,000	500,000	34%
500,000	750,000	37%
750,000	1,000,000	39%
1,000,000	1,250,000	41%
1,250,000	1,500,000	43%
1,500,000		45%

This is all provided for under something called the Estate Tax Credit. According to the Uniform Tax Code, the Estate Tax Credit provides that we may pass a certain amount of our estate to our heirs tax free. This reform came about because there was a large protest among taxpayers regarding high estate taxes and Congress responded at least temporarily by passing the Economic Growth Tax Reconciliation and Reform Act in 2001. Under this legislation, the government provided different tax credits for gifts and estate taxes.

It works in two ways: you can gift anyone—children, relatives, friends—up to $12,000 annually tax free. Then, the Estate Tax Credit also allows you to pass to your children up to $2 million tax free on your death. This figure doesn't count the $12,000 that you may have been giving them annually. So just to be clear, the $12,000 annual gift to your children (or others) does not diminish this $2 million tax credit on your death. In other words, until December 31, 2010, you can give away $12,000 annually tax free and bequeath up to $2 million tax free at your death. But in 2011 this changes *unless* we all start making a fuss to our congressmen and women like others did at the turn of the millennium. As the law stands now, in 2011 you will pay 18 percent in taxes on that same $12,000 gift unless the law is changed.

And just to be really confusing, under the provisions of current law, the Estate Tax Credit has been increasing and the top tax rates have been decreasing until in 2010, where there will be no estate tax at all during that year. If you happen to die in 2010, the estate and gift taxes are repealed and your estate will pay no taxes although your heirs will receive a carryover basis in certain of your assets. ("Carry over" means the original purchase price for the property "carry's over" to whomever the asset was transferred to so whenever the heir sells the property, they will get hit with capital gains tax on the difference between the original purchase price and the sale price of the property.) The following chart shows you what I'm talking about:

Year	Max. Estate Tax Credit	Max. Gift Tax Credit	Max. Unified Rate
2006	$2 million	$1 million	46%
2007	$2 million	$1 million	45%
2008	$2 million	$1 million	45%
2009	$3.5 million	$1 million	45%
2010	Tax Repeal	Tax Repeal	0%
2011	$1 million	$1 million	
2012	$1 million	$1 million	
2013	$1 million	$1 million	

If you survive until 2011, the estate tax bounces back to the 2002 levels. The following chart, which was in place before the Economic Growth Tax Reconciliation Reform Act of 2001 went into effect, shows what the estate and gift taxes will revert to in 2011 unless a new law is passed.

For some reason, our law makers decided that the Gift Tax credit for the years 2006 – 2010 remains at $1 million while the Estate Tax Credit increases from $2 million in 2006 to $3.5 in 2009 with no tax on gifts of any size in 2010. Then, in 2011, it bounces back to $1 million in 2011 and thereafter. I believe that Congress did this to quiet people in the near-term.

As I said above, we can only hope that in 2010 enough people will protest the increased tax rate so

Value or Estate or Gift Exceeding $	Up to	Taxed at %
$0	$12,000	18%
$12,000	20,000	20%
20,000	40,000	22%
40,000	60,000	24%
60,000	80,000	26%
80,000	100,000	28%
100,000	150,000	30%
150,000	250,000	32%
250,000	500,000	34%
500,000	750,000	37%
750,000	1,000,000	39%
1,000,000	1,250,000	41%
1,250,000	1,500,000	43%
1,500,000	2,000,000	45%
2,000,000	2,500,000	49%
2,500,000	3,000,000	50%
3,000,000	10,000,000	55%
10,000,000	17,184,000	60%
17,184,000		55%

Congress will pass another more long-term law that offers a decent solution. But no matter what the table says, it is *vital* that you consult with a tax expert anytime you plan on gifting large amounts of money to your children or others. Tax professionals are paid to keep up with the latest IRS and state tax regulations, and a phone call will save you lots of headaches later.

Prepare Your Map—Know What you Want

Now that we have the tax issues out of the way, we can deal with what I consider the more pressing aspects of planning your estate. Even though I didn't follow my own advice here, estate planning should not be written at a time of high emotion. It should be contemplated, thought out, analyzed, revisited often, and viewed as a continuous financial planning mechanism detached from everyday pressures. It should also be regarded as a vehicle through which you touch the future and impact the lives and families of those you want to benefit. Just as wills and trusts can be helpful, they can also be destructive. The language of your estate plan will either clearly direct your representative regarding your goals, wishes, and plans, or it will abdicate control and decision making to others in the hope that your representative will glean from the language of your trust or will what you really wanted. The old adage, "if you want it done right, do it yourself," applies in many respects to estate planning. It is not a black box, meaning that it isn't something you can't access, change, or even influence. You need only to understand the process, what happens when and how, to understand how much input you really should have. This is essentially the map you're going to leave behind.

More important, however, as you think about setting up your map, consider this: it is always better to have some plan in place rather than no plan at all, for *a mediocre plan well executed beats a brilliant plan poorly implemented every time.* This says it all. An estate plan—the map—is only half of the equation. If you were going on a road trip, you would have a map, but that doesn't tell you how you will actually go about implementing, meaning putting into place, your trip: what you'll pack, what snacks you'll bring, what you'll provide for your children's entertainment (if you are planning on bringing them at all!), where you will stay, in what neighborhood, what and where you will eat. Most people assume that when they create an estate plan, their personal representative will magically know exactly what they wanted and that they will implement it meticulously. In other words, they draw the map but they don't specify the route they want their representatives to take.

I want you to really think about what I'm about to tell you: most trust and estate plans do not account for 70 – 80 percent of the decisions that will be made on your behalf. They can be pages and pages long telling who gets what and when, but it doesn't ever say "how" it is all supposed to happen. It often doesn't even say who gets to make the decision of "when," either, except "in the discretion" of the trustee. Because trust administration can last for years and the assets can be lost or dissipated by multiple forces before they ever get to the beneficiaries, we need to prepare both aspects of the map: the map itself (the initial will or trust) and the route you want your representatives to take (how the will or trust will be administered). There are actually three sides to a trust: its design (the map), its implementation (the route), and its execution (how it all actually plays out). If you have clear directions in the planning and implementation sides, the third side goes a whole lot more smoothly.

A good plan will help a good fiduciary do a good job, but a plan that is linked to a plan of administration will do what the grantor intended and do a better job even with a poor administrator.

Designing Your Map and Your Route

In the design stage of your estate planning, you want to give your representatives clear directions. While we begin first with the "design" of your estate plan, remember the design is integrally linked to its implementation and execution. As you design your plan, do it as though you are guiding your personal representative through the administration of your will or trust. Also, as you design your estate plan, think of it as similar to the financial planning that we do all the time. We make decisions daily with respect to our finances and family, and an estate plan is simply a financial plan projected into the future.

Simple common sense will go a long way in planning for yourself before you even talk to an estate planner; however, recognize that the estate planner is not clairvoyant. He or she does not know you, your family, financial situation, goals, desires or personal relationships as well as you do. No matter what kind of estate planning vehicle you choose, or even if you feel that a will is your best option, there are certain basics questions that every estate plan needs to answer. These questions tell you what needs to go on your map, so no matter if you're just starting the process or reviewing your existing estate document, make sure it answers the following ten questions:

1. Can your assets be located and identified easily?

2. Are your assets in your name alone or owned jointly if married or in some other ownership e.g. partnership, shareholder, etc.? Is a plan in place to segregate your interests from others?

3. Have you updated your will/trust so it is current (within three years)?

4. Have you analyzed the tax liability and administrative costs of your estate and contemplated what should be sold (if necessary) to meet the debts, obligations and tax liability?

5. Have you laid out a plan so your representative can figure out how to implement your wishes?

6. Have you designated someone as your representative (an "executor" for a will and a "trustee" for a trust) who is willing to serve and who will execute your directives in a timely manner consistent with your wishes?

7. Have you identified your beneficiaries so they can be found?

8. Have you taken care of potential claims by third parties against your estate (meaning your creditors)?

9. Have you provided for or disinherited illegitimate or unanticipated heirs?

10. Have you provided a mechanism for resolving disputes

Once you can answer yes to all ten questions, you have solved many of the basic issues that can cause delays and problems in your estate.

Numbers four and ten may need expert help, but you are ahead of the game if you can solve all these issues in your estate plan before you depart this earth. If your answer is no be sure to cure these problems early as they can wreak havoc after you are gone.

If You are Creating a Revocable (Simple) Trust

Remember, a trust differs from a will in that the trustee steps into the grantor's shoes and acts as the grantor, whereas in a will, the executor of the will represents the deceased grantor. In a simple trust, as with a will, the trustee's goal is to pay the debts and obligations of the grantor and to distribute the assets to the beneficiaries. The difference is that a will requires formal court proceedings while the simple trust does not.

As I pointed out in the previous chapter, most simple trusts fall under the subcategory of "revocable" or "living" trust. This is where a simple trust springs to life during the lifetime of the grantor, and the grantor serves as the first trustee. (However, just to keep things straight, a "living trust" is different from a "living will." Learn more at www.suefarley.com.)

As our own first trustee we want to make sure we take care of a whole series of issues that involve our own care, maintenance, and support and additional care during our infirmity or incapacity. Too often we refuse to address these issues until too late. If we had been asked we could have told our children or representative that we really did not want to be institutionalized or placed in a nursing home. Make sure you write down your wishes before the choice is taken from you. Further, because the living trust is usually unsupervised (because we assume we will be in charge until we die; remember this may not be the case), it is important that the people we put in charge of our person and our assets are accountable to us and to our beneficiaries. All too often our trust instrument waives accounting obligations, allowing assets to disappear or be transferred.

Above all, always set your trust up so that it requires your trustee to provide regular accountings and reports. Your trustee should be required to follow probate rules in the preparation of an accounting and report even if it is only to your accountant and attorney or to your beneficiaries. If you've chosen a living trust, you may be told by your estate planner nothing needs to be changed in your normal dealings with your assets. Not so! If you create a living trust, make sure you prepare regular accountings and reports on your activities. Even though you are reporting to yourself, it will require you to become organized, and best of all it sets an example for those who follow. Keeping these records straight is the key to a smooth transition and subsequent administration. It also establishes a standard of care that we can expect our representatives to follow. There is nothing better to follow than the trail of the grantor who has established the procedures he/she wants his/her successors to use by doing the job right from the beginning.

Making others accountable for our money prevents thievery and loss of assets during the period of our infirmity. Accounting and reporting should be annual. It is too easy to allow papers, securities, small assets like jewelry, art, and accounts to disappear when you become infirm. Prepare an inventory of your assets and take pictures. These assets will wind up in your accounting and are part of the reports that you and your successors will prepare annually with copies provided to you and your accountant, attorney, and beneficiaries. As a further reassurance, you can ask your attorney, accountant, beneficiaries, friends, or others to act as an agent to check the accounting and to hold your representative responsible. To this end you may want to sign documents empowering your agent to check on your trustee.

The more questions you answer as to what you want the more guidance your representative will have in making decisions on your behalf. No matter how you put your plan together, make sure you take the time to understand and have input into how your plan will be administered.

The Irrevocable (Complex) Trust

Perhaps the more difficult estate planning instrument and the one that requires more thought, input, and planning is the complex trust. This is the type of trust that does not conclude at death but lasts beyond the grave, sometimes for two to three generations. It requires a more complicated and extensive plan as to how it is to play out and how the goals of the trust are to be reached. Because the planning stage and administrative (the implementation and execution) stage are often segregated by time, the two-parts-to-the-whole frequently do not fit together once they are triggered. If you choose a complex trust, make sure you understand the mechanisms involved rather than simply believing that the assets will be maintained for you and their value will appreciate for use by future generations. Always remember, the people we know today most likely will not be the people who are in charge of our assets and our funds in the future.

In addition to the ten key questions I gave you above, the complex trust requires extensive planning, direction, thought, and grantor input. As you map out this type of trust, be sure to include the following:

1. Anticipate and deal with future events. (I'll go into this aspect more in chapter 3.)

2. Prescribe a thorough and comprehensive reporting mechanism that assures the trustee is actually working for the interests of the trust and not his/her own interests.

3. Incorporate removal provisions allowing the beneficiaries to remove and replace the trustee with 50 percent (or other percentage you choose) support of the beneficiaries. This will protect your trust and beneficiaries from a poorly performing trustee.

4. Provide for termination of the trust and distribution of assets with a high percentage of beneficiary consent e.g. 80 percent, 90 percent or unanimous consent.

5. Provide a procedural road map of "how" you expect your appointed representative to accomplish the goals you have set. Set milestones of performance so the trustee can be monitored.

6. Provide a mechanism for regular distributions not subject to the discretion of the trustee.

7. Provide for concluding the trust when the goals set have been reached. Define when the goals will have been reached. For example, "Upon graduation from graduate school or by age twenty-six, whichever comes

first, 50 percent of my son's proportionate share of trust assets shall be distributed to him."

The benefits of having a clear road map are many. Your beneficiaries tend to be happier, and you minimize the risk that the funds that you set aside will be eaten away slowly by fees and poor performance. Estate tax, administrative fees, attorney's fees, appraiser's fees, accountant's fees, poor investment acumen, poor judgment, and many other factors converge to consume anywhere from 10 – 50 percent of your estate or *sometimes even more* after your death. The longer the money or assets are under the control of others, and especially if there is no one around checking up on the trustee, the more likely it is that the assets will be lost or siphoned off in fees or management costs or will lose value from simple inattention.

Define Your Beneficiaries

All of the above planning really comes down to the two most important aspects in a trust: your beneficiaries and your money. This may seem obvious, but my experience has shown me that all too often, beneficiaries are not clearly defined, and the gray area makes for family upset and even division.

I will delve into the problems and solutions that revolve around beneficiaries in later chapters, but suffice it to say here that you must be crystal clear in your trust who your beneficiaries are and how to contact them. Also, define the people you do *not* want to benefit, e.g. unknown illegitimate children, stepchildren etc. If the beneficiary is a minor, it is vital to specify that the guardian can only act under court supervision and that the guardian must account annually to the court for the assets under their control. This helps protect the funds or gift and the court supervises the distribution to the intended beneficiary. Further, if you have minor children, set the parameters of care and investment you want for your family and assets. Do not leave anyone who is your or your children's representative in the dark as to exactly how you want the children to benefit and when.

There should also be a very clearly laid out plan for your beneficiaries. Again, I will go into this in much more depth in later chapters. For now, just know that you will have to anticipate the timing of your beneficiary's needs. You will also have to set clear parameters around to the use of the trust's funds.

It has been my experience that as much as we all want the use of our assets and funds to be handled as we would direct, we also must recognize that the strings we place on assets also bind the person we want to benefit. Too many strings and conditions strangle the person and the gift creating resentment, frustration, and hatred. Conditions for receipt of benefits should be simple and limited. Recognize that the individual beneficiary wants to be treated with a level of respect for their own wishes and that the benefit should be exactly that, not a stranglehold on the person. Most important, identifying and answering all the pertinent issues concerning your beneficiaries will give a clear road map for the person who is to represent your interests and your estate.

In the End, It's Long-Term Money Management

Trusts, no matter if they are simple or complex, revocable or irrevocable, have to do in greater or lesser degree with money. It is the money that you have in assets and have put aside specifically for your beneficiaries. The final aspect to designing a workable map for your trust is to look at how you want your money managed after you're gone.

Be Practical About What you Can Afford

Our greatest desire may be to benefit our friends and family so their life is easier than ours. Yet our wish list must recognize and be designed to deal with reality. Our own care may dissipate the gift we intended for our beneficiaries. We are all living longer and we should anticipate that we might not have enough to get our grandchildren through college. Whatever your goals do not put together a plan that cannot be accomplished because you lack the requisite funds to make it work. Anticipate the funding requirements of anything you want to do or have your children do. Planning is always better than no planning. It gives the successor your words so the beneficiary can see what was intended and how to accomplish the goals.

What it really all comes down to is one simple question: how much of your heirs' assets are you willing to gamble? Your assets are no longer under your control at death, and it is the trustee or executor, not you, who will make the decisions about how your money is distributed if you have a simple trust, or how it will be invested and then distributed if you have a complex trust. If your wishes are not clear, or if your trust contains a "broad grant of authority" to your trustee, then any money you lose from a poor investment decision is money lost. That is the way it goes, and the real losers are your beneficiaries.

On the other hand if you set goals and parameters for investment decisions and demand at least annual accountability for not only your assets but the investment decisions behind the numbers, your trust or estate is less likely to suffer a significant loss in funds. Investment parameters should be defined, mapped, and specified. If the goal of the trust is to educate the beneficiary, you may want to lock away the funds in a government CD or money market account. The fact that you are not getting market returns also means that you are not willing to risk your child's college education on the stock market. Make sure the parameters for investment of assets of the trust are set by you and broad discretionary authority over assets is eliminated. Also calculate the annual burn of administrative fees and costs. I will discuss this later, but it can be significant.

As technology advances in the area of estate planning, sophisticated software will be able to take you through a mechanism of determining your values so parameters can be set regarding investment. For right now, as you start thinking about planning your estate planning map, it is important to understand and know the whys, where's, and how's as to investment management and decisions with respect to your assets. Your personal representative is accountable to your beneficiaries. Make sure your trust or estate provides a mechanism for determining the decisions behind the numbers.

There's a lot to think about in terms of the money-management issues trusts raise, and I am going to go into more depth about the issues you must be aware of and begin planning for in the next chapter. There I will be talking about identifying your values and goals, and while money management might not appear to be tied to your values, it is.

CHAPTER THREE

Planning Your Route:
Declaring the Definable,
Dealing with the Indefinables

Usually we set up our estate plans because our lawyer told us we needed to. So when we go through the process with them, we don't know that most of what they are dealing with is the complicated tax issues surrounding the estate. When they present us with a plan, more often than not it sits idly in our drawer, waiting like a time bomb to go off when we die. Without careful planning, including discussions with our beneficiaries about what we want and how we have planned, we can unwittingly blind side and frustrate the very people we intended to benefit. They may resent that we have locked up assets out of their reach. They may be antagonistic towards the person we have placed in charge and may disagree with the plan we have set in place. They may fight each other because we left them in the dark as to what we intended and why. So too our administrator may be seeing the document for the first time, but we have not shared our plan with them nor have we given them clear direction as to how we want our estate administered.

Often when we approach our estate planner, we talk simply of our assets, our tax liabilities, and who we want to benefit and when. What we rarely discuss is passing on our values and traditions to our families and heirs. We fail to establish any "standard" that we would want to apply to the way decisions are made on our behalf. We assume the legal standard should be enough, whatever that is. Unfortunately, the legal standard is often vague and undefined leaving important decisions as to how to interpret our wishes to our named representative, or worse, to strangers.

What we really want to do is project our standards into the future for our children and heirs. For example, if you have lived frugally, saving your money and assets for your children, it is likely that you would not want to lose funds to a trustee who does not share your values; or if you regard the term "education" to encompass tutoring and trade school, you would be loathe to find that your trust officer defined "education" as only four years of college. The reason this happens, over and over again, is because we fail regularly to define our values and goals which in turn plays out in a failure to direct decision made by our trustee on our behalf.

Values and Goals: How you make decisions today is a key to thinking about building your estate plan

If you have ever planned a party, wedding, trip, stock purchase, business, or anything else requiring your input, you know your values have a lot to do with the decisions you make. You know what you think is right and good. So why would you think the most important plan you will make for everything you have acquired during your lifetime, the plan you make for the most important people in your life, your family, will magically contain your values? Spelling out our values rarely, if ever, is part of the design process of our estate plans because estate plans are primarily declarative in nature. They state what you want to have happen, but as I've said before they rarely say how it should all play out.

If we are creating a trust that will last beyond our death, we must anticipate at some point in the trust's future that someone who may never have known us will be administering our estate or trust for our family. This is what we should plan for in our trusts, and the only way to do so is by providing your trustee and beneficiaries with some sort of an idea of what you value—what you think is right and good and what you think is bad—so that they can make decisions based on that knowledge.

Defining our goals and values, while it sounds daunting, is actually not that difficult. Your goals simply answer why you are setting up the trust. Values come into play when we look at the way we currently think, act, and make decisions to help us discover how we want those goals to be accomplished.

Goals First

Say you die with $250,000 after taxes, administration, and the myriad of other costs. Where would you want the money to go and why? Have you formulated a goal you want accomplished, e.g., helping your daughter through veterinary school? How long do you want your trust to last? This goes back, in part, to deciding what kind of trust you want. In my case, for example, I want my assets to be distributed upon death; I do not want them to be held in trust for years. However, some people want to create a trust that will take care of their family financially because they are no longer here to see that done. If that is your goal, you need to consider what kind of individual you want your child to become: independent and able to function without your money or dependent upon your funds. Perhaps you want your trust to be a "fail safe" for times of trouble.

It is little recognized that there may very well be a fundamental difference in what our estate planner is selling to us and what we think we are buying. Given the way trusts are currently set up, what we intend to accomplish with the estate planning vehicle often may not accomplish our goals. What are our goals in setting up a particular estate plan? Goals usually fall into several categories. The most common of them are below:

1. Parental—care of family and self
2. Financial control
3. Avoidance of taxes
4. Avoidance of probate
5. Charity

Some trusts are set up to ensure the grantor's children are educated or to help them become self-sufficient. Other goals include supporting your spouse, paying for medical expenses, providing help to a particular charity, or benefiting a friend. Some people, as I pointed out in the previous chapter, want to control their money as long as they can, and that is their main goal for the trust. Others simply want to put their money in a trust to protect it from estate taxes. Still others want to protect their children's assets from fortune hunters and other unsavory situations by protecting the funds and making them available when needed. While tax avoidance is a legitimate goal, you should determine just how your estate and heirs save by the creation of a complex trust. For example, the tradeoffs made for such tax savings may tie up the assets beyond the reach of your heirs for years and be of no value to them. If the trust legitimately saves you and your heirs' money, by all means, use it as a vehicle for this purpose, but don't prolong the trust for generations on this basis alone. Whatever your goals, they should be specific to what you want and how you want them accomplished.

Also, other things to consider as you begin thinking about the goals for your trust include these three essentials:

A. Have you funded the trust with sufficient assets to accomplish your goal and cover the inherent administrative, legal, accounting, and expert expenses that go along with accomplishing that goal? Even though I will go into much more depth in part two about the problems that can happen to your funds while they are in a trust, I just want to point out here that the administrative and legal costs surrounding a trust can consume the trust and hence the goal is never reached.

B. Is there a plan laid out in sufficient detail so someone could accomplish your goal for you? Letting others decide how you want your goals to be accomplished often leaves them with too little guidance and leaves them to make the decisions for you. This leaves your trust vulnerable to misdirection, misappropriation, and never accomplishing the original purpose for the trust in the first place. Also, you should have plan B in place just in case your stated goals are not accomplished or are frustrated in some way.

C. As you plan your goals, you also must consider who will carry out your wishes. Again, I will cover this issue in much more detail in the next two sections of the book, but for now, I just want to point out how important your pick of trustees is to the carrying out your goals. Questions to consider on this issue: Are you counting on family, friends, or professionals to serve as your representatives? What about the possibility that they will not serve? What about the problem that they may have no training as trust or estate administrators? Do you think they will know what to do? In order to clearly define your goals as you are designing your trust, you should plan as if a complete stranger is managing your trust. That way, no matter who is managing your money, whether you know them or not, they will have some sense of how you want the trust to be handled.

Defining the goals of your trust is relatively easy and should be fairly straightforward to your fiduciary, whomever you pick. However, there would still be a great deal of unknowns if you only set forth your goals for the trust because they are still part of the declarative "what" most trusts are made of. So once you have defined your goals, you need to give some idea and direction as to *how* you want your goals to be met. That is done by allowing your trustees and your beneficiaries to know what you value.

Projecting Your Values and Priorities into the Future

"Values" have generally been defined as a set of beliefs of a person or a social group in which they have an emotional investment. For example, if you believe that controlling from the grave is a bad thing, and that your children should reap the benefit of the assets you have left them at your death, this is one of your values.

In order to define your values, you must look into past actions and decisions to discover patterns that become part of your own estate-design tool kit. But in the end, defining values is as simple as figuring out and then writing down what is important to you. You need to consider the value you place on your family, your place of worship, charitable giving, education, recreation, travel, investments, friendships, assets, tradition, the environment, and even your freedom. Whatever you think about all of these different areas of your life must somehow be conveyed in the trust so that boundaries for decision making can be set. You must delve into your own values so you can convey them to your children and grandchildren. And know that these are not just moral values, but real values played out by you in your life every day.

Currently, the most common way that you make your values known are in a document called a "letter of instruction." This is a document that is a catch-all for all the important stuff that is not included in your trust. Right now, letters of instruction usually just set out some of the important yet mundane stuff like bank account numbers, insurance policies, usernames and passwords for Internet accounts, and the like. Some of the better letters I've seen also set out instructions for your heirs on how to claim life insurance policies (while that might seem obvious, grief is very disorienting, and it helps to have these things spelled out.) What I'm advocating is that you also spell out your values—how you think about things like money, health, and education for example. This is how you will set parameters for decision making.

Warning: Unfortunately, few attorneys use this tool today. They argue that letters of instruction create ambiguity and the broad discretion granted to a trusted friend, relative, or professional in the trust itself allows the executor or trustee the flexibility to deal with the assets as they deem, appropriate. Unfortunately, the broad discretion granted makes them the decision maker, not you. Since we do not yet have the sophisticated technology to help track all the elements of a trust, the letter of instruction is the best tool we have right now.

The best way to project your values into the future is to look at how you've made decisions in the past. The following includes the nine most common areas I have identified as where a screening for values must take place:

Technology Teaser

Right now, I am creating templates for letters of instruction to be incorporated into trusts and wills defining terms and setting forth parameters for decision making. These templates can be used to define parameters for each of your beneficiaries.

They are designed to be integrated into your existing will and/or trust and will assist your estate planner in defining what you intend the terms he/she uses to mean. Eventually these will be incorporated into technology that links your trust to an administrative plan defining parameters for decision making.

Review these templates with your estate planner who may incorporate them into your trust and/or will. The estate planner may also choose to define these terms himself/herself in the manner you direct. You can download these letters of instruction at www.SueFarley.com.

Money: Since a trust is about money, it is vital that you tell your trustees and beneficiaries how you value money. Have you saved or spent money on travel, charities, education, family, or yourself? Have you been steadfast in paying the mortgage, insurance, taxes, utilities, and other home expenses? Do you have anything left at the end of the day? The mundane daily maintenance of home and family tells a lot about your own character. It tells that you value your home and family and have assumed a level of responsibility that you would like to see in the people who represent you. These may be the values you want to project in the trust, and it helps your trustee and your heirs understand how the money is distributed. For example, what comes first when you think beyond just making the mortgage payment? If you think first of travel over paying for clothing, furniture, art, or other things, then that says you value personal experience over tangible objects. It gives your trustee an idea of how much latitude you may want to give your trustee when he/she distributes the trust's funds to your children for their own travel. You also want to be very clear about how you value charitable giving. Have you devoted many hours to the local Society for the Prevention of Cruelty to Animals (SPCA) or given money to a local charity, to a religious organization, or to save the environment? By looking at these types of things, you will be better able to formulate exactly what you expect from your administrator or trustee when it comes to distributing your trust's funds.

Health: One of the most common phrases in a trust is that the money is there to support the "health, education, and welfare," of the spouse and the grantor's descendants. But if you have set up a trust with benefits to your spouse and children with directions that the trustee is to take care of the "health, education and welfare," of your family, what does this really mean? If one child becomes ill or is injured in an accident requiring a significant outlay of funds to rehabilitate or maintain the child, what amount or portion of the trust's funds will you make available for this purpose? Are trust funds to be diverted from his/her education fund to his/her medical needs? Does this mean that the college fund for your other child or children is now lost and to be dissipated for the care of the injured or ailing child? By taking a hard look at how you value health, you're in a better position to make decisions for yourself and your family instead of abdicating these important decisions to your representative.

One way to define your values concerning health is to look at what you pay for now: preventative care, dental care, eye care, health insurance for family and children? It is important to note that while you can't plan for everything, clearly identifying how important health and health care is to you can help your fiduciary make decisions concerning your beneficiaries that you did not specifically address but must be dealt with nonetheless

Also, while we're on the issue of health, it is important you learn the difference between a trust and a living will. Just to give you an overview: the living will is set up specifically as a medical directive and can include a financial directive when you may be temporarily incapacitated by surgery or some unforeseen event and you cannot speak for yourself. A living will lets your family and doctors know how you would want life, death, and health decisions made on your behalf. It answers questions such as: do you want to be maintained on life support if you have suffered brain death; what medical treatment you do and do not want, whether you want all medical resources utilized to restore you to health; do you want to die with the help of hospice, etc.? It also identifies your doctors and who is to care for you, your children, and your finances when you cannot speak for yourself. For more information about living wills, please go to my website (www.SueFarley.com). There you will find a more in-depth explanation as well as a sample living will template that you can review with your lawyer.

Education: This is perhaps one of the stickiest areas in a trust because it truly is a hazy area. To illustrate my point, look at this real-life example. I once dealt with a case where the trust provided for the education, support, and maintenance of the child for *"as long as the child remained in school."* One of the beneficiaries as well as the trustee interpreted the provision literally. The problem was that the child became a perpetual student working on his fourth PhD at age thirty-nine! As far as I know, the person is still in school. Is this what the parents intended in setting up a trust for their child's support and education? If the parents had been alive, would they have interpreted this provision the same way as the trustee?

As you think about what to include in your letters of instruction about education, consider what educational decisions you have made for yourself for your own social development. For example, you may have chosen a trade school over traditional college, and so you consider attending trade school a valid form of education. Other questions to ask yourself: what level of education do you have? Was it enough for your life, or do you want to provide for the opportunity for more education for your children? Do you believe your children should work as a condition of receiving benefits from your trust? Would you pay for more than four years of college to allow your children to graduate?

If you have children, you want to make sure that you let your trustee know exactly what you mean by education. The term "education" may mean different things for different beneficiaries. You may have grown children and minor children. Will the term "education" be defined and interpreted in the same manner for each? Or, do you really intend different benefits for each child under the term education? I always advise people to write separate letters of instruction with respect to each child. Separate letters for each child will guide your trust's administrator in the decisions you would make for your family. Know that if you do not provide this type of direction, it is the trustee's decision that will prevail.

Welfare: The term "welfare" is perhaps the murkiest term of all in trusts. It generally means that you are providing for the well-being of your heirs. However, welfare for one could mean a $10,000 a month (or more) stipend, while others would be grateful for anything extra they would get. In other words, "welfare" to one might be "luxury" to another, so it is very important you define what you consider to be the necessities and luxuries of life. And like education and health, the idea of welfare is defined in large part by how you have lived your life. How do you spend your money? What philosophy do you espouse regarding necessities or gifts, and how do you feel you have carried out your own philosophy during your lifetime? Do you have enough to be generous? Will that generosity be appreciated or earned? Are there conditions that should be set regarding the release of funds based on issues of welfare? Is the release of funds and assets linked only to age-related events? Or perhaps you want to match funds with achievements and goals that have been attained? For example, one family created a trust that specified that at age twenty-six, the child would receive in distribution from the trust one-half of what the child earned that year. It is just an example but an important one because it shows where distributions were keyed to performance by the child. On the other hand, support for your spouse may be a completely different standard. If you do have a different standard for your spouse than for your children, have you specified what it is? Again, definitions specific to the beneficiary can be set forth in letters of instruction.

Another area of welfare that most don't consider fully is entertainment. Have you taken vacations, traveled, lived abroad, and participated in social events and functions? Do you want your spouse or your children to have these same experiences? You may believe that such expenses are not to be funded by the trust. Each of these parameters is important for a definition of how you want decisions made later regarding the use of your funds and assets.

Religion/Culture: Whether you have strong religious convictions or have no particular belief system, it is important to convey to your representative a standard for their decision making. Religious and cultural backgrounds are important values that you may want to convey in your trust. While you might not be aware of it, the manner and methods you have used to handle your assets and family decisions often times are influenced to greater or lesser degree by cultural influences and religious beliefs. For example, your religious convictions may be expressed in the form of investments from the trust, e.g. no company that funds embryonic research will receive trust funds. Or, it may take the form of promoting a particular education with funds being provided for a journey to Israel.

Relationships: Relationships are important to deal with before your estate plan is implemented. Identify who and how you want to benefit the people or entities you name as beneficiaries. Make sure that your representative can find your beneficiaries. For entities that you name as beneficiaries, identify them in detail, where they are located, their headquarters, and even the name of a person with whom you have most frequently dealt. This will save your estate thousands of dollars spent by your trustee trying to discover this information.

While this seems to be relatively straightforward, this subject is often anything but. Relationships are complicated. Family relationships are even more complicated. As I have noted before, relationships now must often take into account social alliances. These can be in the form of multiple marriages, out-of-marriage relationships, same-sex relationships, and children from any of the above. If you don't clearly define who is to benefit, it can be one of the major land mines in your trust waiting to explode. Your entire estate can be wiped out as potential heirs' battle it out over your assets. Even if you have no bad feelings, rivalries, or hatreds, they can be planted by your trust for generations to come through your failure to enlighten your beneficiaries regarding your plan and dealing with these issues before you die.

I also find that while grantors may think they can just ignore sticky, even explosive issues, they shouldn't. The extramarital affair, illegitimate children, adopted versus natural children, drug abuse, and criminal activities, all must be dealt with by someone, so better you than a stranger.

I will discuss in later chapters how some decisions with respect to families seem to work better than others, but for now, suffice it to say that the estate plan should be designed to foster unity rather than promote or perpetuate dysfunction and rivalry.

Spouse/Significant Other: It is important to seriously consider how you want to benefit your spouse. How did you treat them during marriage? Did they work? Did they and can they financially support themselves when you are gone? Did you contribute to their support financially, and are they dependent upon continued support? There are certain tax advantages that the spouse enjoys, so you should learn as much about them as you can and take advantage of them. Your estate planner will tell you the ins and outs of the tax benefits of certain plans. Ask questions of your estate planner sufficient so you understand what benefits you get and the tax ramifications of each gift. And as always, it is important that you know about the tax advantages and disadvantages of a plan before you commit to it. (If you didn't catch it before, go to www.SueFarley.com where I define the different trusts available to you and the tax situations each present.)

Other questions to consider and define in your trust include: whether your spouse is to receive assets and funds outright or are they left a life interest? (A life interest means you get to use the asset(s) for your lifetime and then upon your death, it goes to someone else. It is very typical to give a life interest in your house, for example, to your spouse, and then when he/she dies, it goes to your children. This guarantees that if the spouse remarries, he/she cannot then give your home to his/her next spouse, leaving the kids out of luck.) Are there multiple marriages involved that could impact the benefit and subject it to dispute? Benefits that you give to your spouse may place him or her in conflict with your children. For example, if you provide "income" to your spouse from property you own and the children are to receive the asset when he/she dies, the children may wind up in conflict with the way the spouse is managing or maintaining the house. There is often a tug-of-war between a push for benefits by the children who want the funds for education, starting a business, or buying a house and a pull by the spouse who needs the funds to survive. It should be you who decides how to resolve this type of dispute. Make sure you include priorities, e.g. whose needs come first and a dispute-resolution mechanism.

If you are in an out-of-marriage or same-sex relationship, in most states you are not treated the same as if you were married. (Also, live-in partners are generally not considered relatives.) More contractual protections are in order.

Children: Even though I've already discussed beneficiaries in chapter 2, it is important to revisit the topic of one of the main beneficiaries of any trust—your children. It is important for you to examine the values you have concerning your children. Depending upon their age, children need varying degrees of education, support, and protection. To have a child means not only an emotional commitment but a financial and social commitment for a minimum of eighteen years. For the young child less than eighteen years of age, food, shelter, financial support, education, and a skilled someone to implement all of the above is critical. Yet beyond these most basic needs is a social, religious, and cultural structure in which your child will be raised. Most parents want to have input into these factors as well. Even after age eighteen, the spectrum of college education, room, board, graduate school, and first job still remain in the arena requiring parental input and assistance. We do not own our children; we are given the gift of time to spend with them to nurture their growth, teach them to survive, and value themselves and others. Part of the time we spend on them must include planning their future.

Know that if you die leaving a minor and no trust, the court will appoint a guardian to raise your child. If you have a will you may choose a guardian but the funds and assets that belong to you will be held or spent by your child's guardian in a manner deemed appropriate by them. You will have no input into this process. On the other hand if you create a trust, you may direct the trustee to take certain actions defined by the trust. You simply have more input and direction in terms of your child through a trust. Make sure you think through who you want to raise your child in your absence. Consider what will be required for your child's support, maintenance, health, education and welfare and plan in detail providing a map of what you want.

How you make decisions for your children now establishes boundaries and parameters for future decisions by your trustee. Because the technology to assist you is currently unavailable, you must prepare letters of instruction that are as clearly defined as possible. Then, when the technology does come on line, the boundaries of administration you have set can be established into an electronic system when it is available.

> **Technology Teaser**
> Technology will allow us to project our values, wishes, and decisions into the future. When it becomes available, it is vital that we take advantage of this sophistication to plot the boundaries for acceptable and unacceptable use of our funds and assets.

Bloodline: How well do you know the people you wish to benefit? Do you have enough assets to benefit more than one generation? These are the two intertwined issues in terms of bloodline. The average trust today is $1.1 million in assets. Despite the original purchase price of our homes, many of us have close to this amount or more in assets simply by reason of the appreciation of real property acquired. Depending upon the number of people in your family, $1 million may benefit more than one generation. But as you set up a complex trust, the only kind of trust that can accommodate multiple generations, you must be very clear on the issue of bloodlines.

Who do you consider your heirs or beneficiaries? People often regard bloodlines as very important, but this is an area that causes more problems than I can articulate in this book. Adopted children are not related by blood. Does this matter? To some it matters a great deal.

As you delve into defining your values about bloodlines, you need to think carefully about whether you want to create unity in your family or perhaps unknowingly perpetuate family division. The successful estate plan sets the family up to succeed. It deals with issues that during one's life may have created problems and division. It does not perpetuate these divisions. When I'm asked for advice, I always say, "You should plan to be better than you are." Take the high road in the decisions you make. In other words, assume the viewpoint that wrongs that were visited upon you during your life belong to you alone; they do not belong to your children. Your children will have enough of their own baggage without carrying yours. Anticipate issues and deal with them in advance.

Take this case as an example. In one family, the patriarch created a trust that benefited his children, his grandchildren, and their children. The grantor divorced his first wife leaving her with three children. He remarried and his second wife became pregnant. Not wanting additional children, the grantor and the newly married second wife separated over the pregnancy. The grantor eventually reunited with his first wife. Despite the fact that the fourth child (child of the second marriage) should have been treated equally by the grantor under his trust, the other beneficiaries refused to treat this fourth child as an equal. Even though the child of the second marriage had nothing to do with the choices of his father, he and his heirs suffered for generations being tied to people who regarded them as "the bastard side of the family." The fourth child was viewed by the first wife's three children as undeserving of any benefits from the father. He was treated with disdain and condemnation by relatives who resented his interest in properties owned by them all. The first wife's children perpetuated the ill feelings of their mother and used it as a means of taking advantage of the child of the second marriage. The father could have anticipated this division and provided separately for the second wife's child.

While many want their bloodline to benefit from their efforts and receive their assets and family wealth, it is important to look at situations in your family that may place your children and family members at odds. If you can anticipate these events, you can plan a method that works rather than having people artificially aligned for generations, promoting division and hatred for generations.

In the case I just mentioned, if the grantor had simply segregated the interests of the beneficiaries as well as included in the trust a method for resolving disputes, his beneficiaries could have avoided years of dysfunction.

The upshot to all this is, empower your beneficiaries to segregate their interests from the whole and give them the option of having their own separate trusts when you can expect that the parties may not get along.

Money Management and Values

In chapter 2, I ended with a promise that we would take up the matter of managing your money in this chapter. We're now back to that point and I hope you can see managing your money has everything to do with your goals for the trust and the values by which you have lived your life. Most of us know how we have handled the assets under our control. However, do you think that your personal representative will handle your assets in the same manner after you are gone? The answer is no, especially if no clear directions are given. The usual case is that once you are no longer around to shepherd the assets you have accumulated, you should anticipate they will not be treated in the same manner. Whomever you name as your "trusted" investment advisor generally behaves very differently once you are gone. You should also anticipate that your beneficiaries will not have the investment acumen that you possess. It is completely possible that the assets you worked so hard to accumulate during your lifetime will not be preserved by your representative after your death and in fact may be dissipated in fees, costs, expenses, etc.

In order to best assure your assets are being managed in a manner consistent with your wishes, it is important to have established a plan that encompasses your personal values and directives. The best way to start getting that all down on paper is to anticipate some of the events that could happen and consider how your assets should be managed under those circumstances.

Anticipate Events

When we create our will or trust, we must anticipate events, events that carry with them a high impact to the trust but low probability of occurring as well as the low-impact but high- probability events. For example, say you have three children and have enough money to send them to college. You set up a trust for this purpose with perhaps a little extra money, and you feel complacent that the plan is in place. But what happens to those funds if one of your children is sucked into the drug scene and requires funds for rehabilitation and counseling? Are the funds available for this rather than college? Would you take funds from your other children's college funds to save one of your children from spiraling into drug use? What if that child is saved but will require substantial financial support, rehabilitation, retraining, and assistance for the rest of his/her life? Will you take the college funds from your other two children and redirect them to the child who is suffering?

Here's another less-dramatic situation I've seen play out. The grantor had several children and had funded the trust with just enough money to cover the education and support for each child through four years of college. The son had done well in college, but at the end of four years didn't have enough units to graduate. Here's the question: should the trust pay for a fifth year of college to assure the son's graduation, knowing that the funds for college for the other children would be depleted by perhaps $50,000.00? No matter what happened, someone was going to suffer. In this case, one of the other children was only funded for three years of college under the trust. Should the trustee have cut off the fifth year of benefits?

Other cases I've handled had to do with the hard but true fact that most of the time, our children are not created equal. What do you do when one has a learning disability but another wants to be a doctor which requires expensive graduate school training, and another still wants to start her own business with the funds from the trust? These are decisions that would test the Wisdom of Solomon. Yet in many instances, because the grantor failed to anticipate future events, these decisions are left to the discretion of the trustee.

As you anticipate events, you take into account your value system, and then set priorities in your trust that work. This is sometimes not an easy task as it brings into play the entire history or your relationships with others and even your perspective on life. Anticipating events also depends upon your circumstances, age, wealth, number of people you want to benefit, and circumstances of the beneficiaries. But, the bottom line is, we know our families and assets better than our estate planner. Rather than abdicating decision making to our estate or trust administrator, we should anticipate events and tell them how we would decide the issue.

Now there is a caveat to all of this. If you decide to have a will or simple trust, the number of events you will have to anticipate will be less than those if you decide you have sufficient assets to create a complex trust that will last for several generations.

Most important, no matter which type of trust you choose, plan for yourself as well. There should be direction from you, either in the trust instrument itself or in a "letter of instruction," detailing how you want to deal with your own infirmity, subjects like the following:

1. How and where you want to be cared for in your old age.
2. What care do you want if you cannot speak for yourself, and it is temporary? (e.g. nursing, food preparation, housing, financial services and oversight etc.
3. Who do you want to care for you, and will they serve? If you cannot find someone, then who?
4. How do you want your assets treated, e.g., sold and distributed or transferred in an undivided interest to your heirs before your death?
5. How do you want your beneficiaries to receive the benefits you bestow. Are there items that cannot be divided that you wish to remain in the family?

6. How you expect the estate taxes to be paid e.g., sale of which assets, liquidation of what stock, etc.?

7. To whom will your caregiver account for your care? Who will secure your assets? Who will pay your bills?

8. What type of reporting requirements do you expect? Who will deal with your doctors, dentists, bankers, household help etc. for you. To whom do they account?

9. Guardianships for your children. Who will take care of them if you die suddenly? Do you have a plan for your minor children?

10. How are you dealing with life-insurance benefits that will go to your minor children? Have you put safeguards in place to assure the money will be there when they need it? Do you have someone who will make the necessary claims against the insurance company on behalf of your children? Who have you placed in charge of your children's money?

11. Anticipate family disputes and provide a dispute-resolution formula.

12. If you have a family business, is it to be dissolved or continue? Who will be in charge and what parameters have you set for its continued operation?

13. Anticipate what will happen to your assets, car, boat, jewelry, stocks, bonds, home, ranch, cattle, apartment, commercial property, etc. Do not just hand it over, expecting it to be preserved. Give your representative a plan as to how you would want to deal with each asset. List your assets so others do not have to search for this information.

14. Funeral, burial, and the type of service you would like. Plan for where you want to be buried, cremated, entombed, etc.

15. Living will in case you may be terminally ill or in a vegetative state.

16. Who will speak for you when you cannot speak for yourself either from illness or old age?

17. Spell out exactly whom you want to benefit and those you do not want to benefit.

18. Ensure you clearly define the terms in your trust that are subject to multiple interpretations: health, education, maintenance, support, welfare, manage, invest, dispose, etc. Provide a map for each beneficiary and each asset providing parameters for administration.

19. Set parameters against which your trustee's performance can be measured, and if they fail to perform, provide a removal mechanism that is cheap, quick, and does not involve litigation.

20. Set parameters for investment goals and how to reach them; provide that there is accounting for all of it.

While this list is long, it's not inclusive. A grantor's "anticipated events" list can only be driven by the grantor's wants, desires, assets, and beneficiaries. Only the grantor has the capability of answering the above questions; however, if you read them closely, you'll find they cover many of the questions concerning values I gave you above. You are welcome to use this list as a guide to help you form your own "anticipated events" list.

If you find that creating a list is difficult, one helpful way to anticipate events is to ask your prospective representatives how they would decide these issues for you. I tried this out myself with my daughter. I asked where she would bury me. She went on that I would be buried in the ground on a hill overlooking a view. I would become part of the earth. Well, this may sound nice to her, but I do not want to be buried in the ground. The thought of the dampness and worms and such consuming me creates a picture I want no part of. It is now clear to me that I should make this directive clear, or better yet, pick out my final resting place and arrange for it myself. It is important to deal with all these issues over time, methodically addressing the issues that matter to you.

Values Set Standards

In virtually every state, any person placed in a position of trust and named as trustee or executor, particularly a professional fiduciary, is required to act at all times solely in the interest of the beneficiaries. (It's called the Duty of Loyalty.) They must administer the trust or estate in accordance with its terms, purposes, and interests of the beneficiaries (the Duty of Administration). They are required to take steps to protect the property of the estate or trust (the Duty of Control and Protection of Trust or Estate Property) and maintain clear and accurate records of their administration (the Duty to Keep Property Separate and Maintain Adequate Records). Where there are two or more beneficiaries, the trustee executor must act impartially in investing, managing, and distributing trust property (the Duty of Impartiality). The trustee or executor is required to enforce the claims of the trust and/or estate and defend claims against the estate or trust (the Duty to Enforce and Defend). They are to report and account to the beneficiaries (the Duty to Inform and Report).

But do trustees and administrators always follow these rules? Not really. Very simply, most people who are entrusted with administering a trust have little knowledge of the applicable laws, have no oversight, and no standards set by the trust documents to follow. Part of the problem, too, is that many trustees and administrators are family members, and may have no idea that laws exist about administering a trust, let alone how to apply them. The professional fiduciary knows these rules exist but frequently does not apply them because they are costly and time consuming. As I will discuss at length in the next part of the book, many factors cloud the administration of an estate or trust, including the self-interest of the trustee or administrator. Investments that kick back fees to the administrator or trustee may be more attractive to him or her than to financial instruments that have no such benefit.

So, without standards against which to measure performance, it is very difficult to enforce the rules and laws associated with trusts.

In the case of the family trustee, there is no supervision of the trust, and so if the trust is not clear about how to distribute the funds, then the beneficiaries are the ones who lose. For the professional trustee, the Federal Deposit Insurance Company (FDIC) and Office of the Comptroller of the Currency (OCC) are supposed to supervise but really have no capability of overseeing compliance with the trust's terms. Again, I will go into detail about the many problems in a trust in the next part of the book. But for now, just be aware that if you don't set standards for performance, based on your goals and values, you risk losing everything you've saved for your family.

Oh and don't feel complacent about it all, thinking you can simply turn to the courts to help. I encounter individuals all the time who feel satisfied that they have set up their will or trust adequately and simply reply to my warnings: "But the beneficiaries have a right to sue; everything is written down." This naïveté is why this book was written. The beneficiaries often do not have the resources available to them to sue, and the fact that things are written down becomes meaningless where there is not enough knowledge and resources to enforce the will or trust. And all too often, fear is instilled in the beneficiaries that their source of benefits will be cut off if they challenge the actions of their representative upon whom they depend for funds.

Set Parameters and Constraints to Protect your Assets

As I mentioned above, most if not all trusts are declarative. They tell you who is to receive the benefits, when they are to be received, and the purpose for providing such benefits. But the only direction they give to the administrator comes in the form of language like the following:

> *The trustee shall have the following powers in addition to those now or hereafter conferred by the statutes of (state): (1) to retain any property originally constituting the trust or subsequently added thereto, to continue to operate a business, and to invest and reinvest the trust property in bonds, stocks, mortgages, notes, bank deposits, options, futures, limited partnership interests, shares of real estate investment trusts and registered investment companies or other property of any kind, real or personal, domestic or foreign; the trustee may retain or may any investment without liability, even*

> *though it is not of a type, quality, marketability or diversification considered proper for trust investments...*

You may read through this and be overwhelmed because you don't understand, and so you say "so what," but the "so what" is this: this language allows the trustee to gamble with your money and assets because there is no specific language to tell him to do otherwise. On the administrative side, this language means that the trustee may make poor investment decisions for your estate and completely deplete your estate or trust of its assets by playing the futures market with no liability, leaving your heirs with nothing. You will not be around to see that your assets have been kept intact or whether the trustee's interpretation of the above words worked out well. Nor do you know whether the person you have placed in charge of your assets has the requisite skills and training to properly manage the assets of your trust.

Here is a perfect example of how important it is to think about your goals and values before setting up a trust. If, for example, you set up a fund for your children to go to college, there are a variety of questions you should answer. This ensures not only that the funds will be there when they are needed but the parameters of what you intend the trust to pay for are in place. If your child is ten, and you set up a trust with $150,000 to pay for the child's college, you have eight years before the fund will be needed. If you are the trustee for your children, then you may want flexibility. But if you die suddenly, the parameters you have set for yourself, as written in the trust, will be adopted by your successor. Your appointed representative may not possess the business acumen you demonstrated, and he probably doesn't have the same value structure around money as you do. So, with fees, taxes, poor investments, and third parties like lawyers and accountants, that $150,000 could be depleted to $80,000 or much less in eight years when it is time to pay tuition. Since private colleges today require a minimum of about $52,000 per year to pay for tuition, room, board, and expenses, only one year of the college education would be available to your child. Hence, it is important to put constraints on how your successor trustee can invest the original $150,000. You must also anticipate that administrative fees and even taxes will be taken from this fund for the eight-year period of administration.

The trustee's administrative fees, if it is a professional fiduciary, are usually 1 – 1.5 percent of the value of assets under management, or $1,000 to $1,500 annually. Yet beware; the fees tend to be significantly greater than this. The FDIC recently reported that for 2004, deductions for fiduciary fees were a whopping 6.6 percent with an additional 5.1 percent deduction for attorneys, accountants, and tax preparation. This was for trusts' and estates' fiduciary returns, but this is just an average. That means that your trust could be depleted by 11.7 percent annually just in fiduciary fees, attorneys fees, accountants fees, and tax preparation. With this kind of drain on funds, the money may not be available after eight years to fund college. Sure, you say, but the money will be earning interest. Will your trust earn an interest return of more than 11.7 percent? It is unlikely!

The moral of this story is simply, set parameters for your trustee and, if possible, for the fees they will charge; have input into the investment strategy and set benchmarks for performance. (For example: if this same fund sat in a 3 – 4 percent savings account with no administration the funds would still be there.)

If your investment strategy allows discretionary investment, define the parameters of investment. Don't just say, "I want my funds to be invested in stocks and bonds," say specifically which type of stocks and bonds. Make sure you specify the rating of the investment instruments, the expected rate of return and when to sell. The people you relied on for your own financial success will most likely not be around for your children or your children's children. Define the limits of investment and give parameters for fees that may be charged. In short it is simply *not okay* for all of your assets to wind up in the pockets of the administrators, lawyers, and other professionals to resolve issues you should have addressed yourself.

Recognize and Establish Value-Oriented Rules

Most administrators and trustees welcome some direction from the grantor on any of the subjects the trust addresses. To be fair to them, they are often extremely frustrated by the lack of direction and the decisions they have to make that place them at odds with the people they are to represent. However, when things go wrong, they would rather blame their actions on the grantor, and perhaps they have a point.

We need to take responsibility for the trusts and estates we create, and to do that, we must use our own values to spell out how assets will be managed, funds used, family members cared for, etc. Don't depend on the law to do it for you. While the law itself provides a certain standard and value system we expect our trustees and administrators to follow, what I call the "default standard," it is normally costly to enforce. For example, there is no readily established standard of care for the "maintenance" of your spouse. You may say, "Maintain her in her accustomed manner of living," what does that mean? The accustomed manner of living may have very different meaning for the wife, the trustee, and the other beneficiaries who all share in what is left. Define what you mean based on your values, and attach it to your will or trust in the form of a letter of instruction.

Furthermore, while the law provides rules that govern our fiduciaries, enforcement of those rules is a daunting task. First, the beneficiary must recognize that there is a breach for which there is a remedy at law. Because all records are maintained by the fiduciary, the beneficiary may not discover error or wrongdoing with respect to his/her trust or estate until the loss has already occurred. Once the breach is discovered, the beneficiary's sole remedy, short of voluntary correction by the errant fiduciary, is a lawsuit, and this is *precisely what I want you to avoid.* Why? Because these battles tend to take years, they are devastating to the family involved, and the cure can often cost more than the ailment.

Save yourself the heartache and the expense. Designing a trust right can minimize errors, and that means the money you set aside in your trust can be used for its intended purpose: benefiting your beneficiaries.

PART TWO
Trusts are Untrustworthy: Confronting the Problems with Trusts

Towards the end of part one, I started hinting more and more about the various problems that arise in trusts. After thirty years of seeing the different problems that trusts have, I can safely say that no aspect of the industry is safe. The trust system, as it is currently set up, is simply untrustworthy. We have come to rely on the integrity of those we place in charge but there are too many forces that undermine the system.

As I pointed out in the introduction, it is a trillion dollar industry. In 1991 Boston College released a study *Millionaires and the Millennium*, which, on the low side estimated an inter-generational wealth transfer of $41 trillion over the next fifty years. A lot of people want a piece of that very large pie, but all of the entities involved in making a trust—the grantors, estate planners, the trustees, and the beneficiaries—refuse to really take a hard look at all the problems that abound in a trust. Each entity looks at the trust from their own perspective, but this can be blinding for everyone. They can't see the forest for the trees, as the old saying goes. But in stepping back to look at the forest instead of the trees, we can point to areas that consistently have problems from generation to generation.

When you look at the full "life cycle" of a trust as I have, you start to see why and how they go wrong. As you know by now, the problems that arise with trusts begin in the design stage. They don't include the important information they need to direct the trustees at the administrative stage. There are, in fact, three stages to a trust:

design, implementation, and execution. We've talked at length about the design, and I've started giving you guidelines that handle the implementation aspect, the how-to part of a trust. However, it is really only in the execution stage, when the trust goes into effect and when the trustee has to make the tough decision about which beneficiary gets what benefit (and if it is a complex trust, how to invest the funds), that the problems in the first two stages actually surface.

Trusts are no longer simply about how you want to give your money and stuff away, and they are no longer just a problem for the rich. And here's the irony to all of this: these problems have been attached to trusts for a long, long time, but because trusts used to be what only the super-rich did with their money, we didn't really care if the system was untrustworthy. We figured they probably had money to lose and could hire the lawyers to fight the system if they needed to. So no one has really been paying attention, but the problems have continued to grow. The entities associated with trusts, the estate planners and the professional fiduciaries, are all aware that the system does not work well. But when they attempt to fix the problems, they focus on their segment of the industry rather than looking at the life cycle of the trust as a whole. They never seem to get that the problems begin with the trusts themselves. So when the fiduciaries get the beneficiaries to waive their rights as a condition to accepting their trusts (a "fix" the professional fiduciaries have put into place), and then do a bad job, well, it wasn't their money anyway. In order to fix the problems with trusts, the whole trust ecosystem, as it were, needs to be overhauled. What you're about to read will probably—hopefully—shock, anger, and annoy, you. Even though you're about to find out some of the ways you could be legally bilked out of your money, know that there are viable solutions. You can maintain control of this process.

CHAPTER 4

Estate Planning Problems:
What your Lawyer Does and Doesn't Know Can Hurt You

Just recently I had a woman call me frantically, asking for my help. She had read an article in the local newspaper and had been trying to find me. She and her husband were in the process of putting together their trust, and the bank they were working with wanted them to sign all sorts of waivers. The wife didn't want to, but her husband kept insisting that she do it just so the process could be over. She was smart. She smelled a rotten egg in those waivers, and by not signing them, she saved herself and her heirs untold amounts of grief—and lost cash. However, most of the people who come to me aren't so proactive. By the time most people get to me, it's often too late. The banks, lawyers, family members, third parties, and others have moved in. They are in complete control of the trust's funds, and the person's money has been lost or the family farm is about to be lost. It's from these stories that I write this chapter about the fallout from problems people have had to deal with in terms of their trusts.

Having handled trust cases for the past twenty-seven years, I can safely say I have never seen the same story twice. Each problematic trust that comes across my desk is unique. However, I can also say there are broad categories of problems which remain consistent: estate planners not paying attention to the terms they use in the trust document; the trust having no clear map drawn for the trustees to follow in terms of how the assets are being distributed; and trustees, professional and personal not acting as they should. What's most interesting to me is that most of the time people seek my help not because there's been some egregious wrong, but because there's a series of "misdemeanors." Granted, sometimes I get whoppers to deal with, like lawyers who write themselves into the trusts as the trustees and then take off with all the money in the trust. No, it's actually more insidious than that. It's the little errors and incidents that add up over time, the kinds of things that, if it had happened only once, it would not be sufficient to warrant a lawsuit. It's the bank not responding to a beneficiary's request for documentation on the investments made in the name of the trust. It's the family member who won't account. It's the professional or family fiduciary being arrogant and giving their trust clients or beneficiaries the run around. People come to me for help when these little errors become consistent over years, and they start to see a pattern of chronic negligence but don't know what to do.

So while this chapter is all about the reasons why you should *not* trust the trust system as it is currently handled, I also want to empower you with solutions. Above all, you should pay attention to the documents you sign and the people and entities you put in charge. Yes, there are laws on the books that are meant to protect the beneficiaries, but the only people who can enforce those laws are the beneficiaries. Sometimes their hands are tied because the grantor didn't do a good job of setting the trust up right. Sometimes they can't do anything about their rapidly depleting trust because the only way they can sue for damages is hire attorneys out of their own pocket, and they may not have the funds to do this.

To prevent any of this from happening to you, I'm going to take you through the problems trusts contain by starting at the beginning with your estate planner, moving into the various areas and issues that create problems, and then ending with the dense forest of ambiguous language that trusts contain. The next chapter will delve into the problems specific to your trustees, whether a bank or a private representative.

Estate Planner Problems

The estate-planning process may take anywhere from three to thirty hours or more, depending upon the complexity of the assets, the grantor's involvement, and the nature of the plan. Yet once the estate plan is complete, the planner's work is finished. Short of a later amendment to the document, there is nothing further for him/her to do. The estate planner is expected to anticipate certain contingencies and events and plan for them. Yet estate planners like to customize their trust and estate plans to themselves. Many use language that can only be understood by the drafter and define or fail to define difficult terms on the assumption that everyone is on the same wavelength.

Because the planning process is usually disconnected from the administrative process, there is no coordination of how the grantor's goals or wishes will actually be accomplished. Many times the people designated to take charge have never seen the document prior to its implementation and have had no opportunity to clarify issues with the grantor, which they are now left to solve. When the document springs to life, usually at our death, all the ambiguities that exist with all the possible interpretations of the words also spring to life, what these words mean at this stage can be the subject of thousands of dollars in litigation if the beneficiaries don't agree with the trustee's interpretation. Of course, what the grantor meant by it all is forever lost since he/she is no longer around to enlighten the person administering the trust.

It is simply a fact that estate and trust documents are often inadequately constructed and critical information is left out or poorly specified. This problem is compounded by the fact that each trust or estate lawyer seems to have a different formula or definition they seek to incorporate. A simple example is language that specifies that the assets are to be "divided equally between the children of the grantor." First, the word "children" often is not adequately defined. As I pointed out in the last chapter, does it include biological children exclusively, or does it include adopted children? What about illegitimate children? Does the term include stepchildren not adopted by the grantor? Then there's the word "equally." What does it really mean? What about that diamond ring or the piano that cannot be cut in two? What if the beneficiaries each want the same item? Has a process been established for a division of assets that will be fair? Sure the item can be sold and the proceeds divided, but did the grantor want that item to be kept in the family or simply sold at auction?

In one of the cases I came across, the grantor left his real property to one trust, the building built on the real property to another trust, and the leasehold of the building to a third trust. In later documents, a transfer of property was described as a sale of the "leasehold premises." This caused huge headaches because it was never clearly defined whether the lease or the land was sold. Because of the lack of specification, the trust may not reflect the true intentions of the grantor and, by default, grants to the trustee or administrator too much freedom in the interpretation of the trust's terms.

But who's really at fault here? Because there are a myriad of assumptions made by both the estate planner and grantor in the planning process, when the grantor dies, the stage is set for disputes to erupt. Fault for the dispute usually goes in all directions

Even something as seemingly straightforward as an estate that is supposed to go to the grantor's grandchildren can be frustrated because the trust can only play out if the grantor's children have children themselves. If they don't have children, this contingent interest fails and the trust gets tied up in expensive litigation. Again, the grantor could, and even should, be proactive and think of these contingencies; however, the estate planner also needs to be proactive and plan for this eventuality.

You may think the above examples are too simplistic and would never happen, but these are real examples that cost tens of thousands of dollars in attorney's fees and litigation to cure. Unanticipated and unaddressed issues can and do complicate the administrative process. One beneficiary of a simple trust expressed her frustration that the planning process was relatively simple, but the administrative process was "hideous" and "people had no idea what they were in for." She didn't realize the problems started in the actual planning of the trust long before her parent's death.

The general problem with estate planning is that it only addresses the disposition of assets and certain tax characteristics surrounding the methods of disposition. Estate planners fail to address "how" the trust will play out. They believe that this is usually left to the discretion of the trustee. They never find out otherwise because the truth of the matter is, the estate planners do not administer the estates they write. Because they rarely see the results of their handiwork, they never know the extent of the problems their documents create. So too, the simple passage of time between creation and implementation allows for events to occur that can alter the reality of the estate plan. Additional children can be born, diluting the interests of some beneficiaries. The law can change; currently the tax laws change annually, and other estate laws change at the rate of about 20 percent per year. Tragic events such as hurricanes, floods, and earthquakes can destroy assets. Family situations change. Divorce and remarriage carry with them their own set of problems. For these and other reasons, the estate planner rarely sees whether his or her plan plays out as expected.

However, there are things you can do to ensure that your estate plan works, works better, and avoids the pitfalls of a poor plan. The best prevention you can put in place right now is to be aware that estate planners simply don't plan both for the implementation and the execution stages of your trust or estate. You have to be proactive. You have to be steadfast in your insistence that your goals and values be included in the trust. You have to anticipate events, hard as that may be, and you must think about how the trust is to be executed. Then you must insist that your estate planner plan your trust accordingly. Since the entire book really is about this very subject, I'm not going into detail here. However, there is one very important point that I do want to make about estate planners:

Avoid Conflict of Interest

Some estate planners name themselves as the trustee of the trust they draft. There are legal prohibitions in many states precluding the trust planner from filling the role of its administrator, and most estate planners stay out of this role. However, there are those who don't, and because of that, inevitably, the grantor and the beneficiaries are the ones who suffer. In one instance, I know of a woman who didn't want to sue her lawyer because she kept hoping he would replenish the trust with the money he had taken and stashed in the Cayman Islands in one of his own corporate entities. He kept promising to put the money back and her rationale was she would never recover if he was in jail. I'm afraid she hopes in vain of ever seeing her money again.

However, the damage caused by a planner who is also the trustee can be far more insidious. I know of one trust where the grantor named the attorney in charge of his trust as trustee. Once the trust was signed, the trustee had complete control of the assets, including the grantor's house. The lawyer, now named trustee, proceeded to take out a $1.5 million loan against the grantor's house. The couple did not know of the loan as they were no longer on title. The trustee took the money and invested it in his own company and put the remaining proceeds in offshore accounts. The couple only learned of the problem when foreclosure proceedings were instituted by the mortgage holder for nonpayment of the debt. Today, the couple is still struggling to unwind an irrevocable trust and recover monies that are long gone. They are also now financially strapped due to large legal expenses and court costs which they have to pay out of their pocket since the trustee/lawyer has control of their assets placed in trust. The couple no longer has any assets they can call their own.

No matter what your lawyer tells you, if he or she is jockeying for the trustee position, don't give in. If a lawyer names himself or herself as the trustee, he can write the trust in such a way that he gives himself unlimited powers over the assets of the grantor. I've also seen trusts where lawyers have written themselves in as beneficiaries. This, too, is improper. It not only violates the rules of ethics of most states, but it places the lawyer in a position to compete for benefits with other named beneficiaries.

Another major conflict-of-interest problem that can occurs is where the attorney makes errors in the drafting of the trust instrument itself. The self-appointed lawyer/trustee or administrator is unlikely to recognize or disclose the mistakes he or she made and instead may attempt to cover them up for fear of their own liability.

So I cannot stress this enough. *It is generally a bad idea to allow the drafter of the will or trust to also be the trustee, administrator, or beneficiary.*

Other Problem Areas

The disconnect between the design of the trust and its administration lends itself to additional problems that don't necessarily fall on the estate planner's head. Because the setup of a trust is so closely tied to how you live your life and what you value, your desires and wishes can often create problems for the very people you intend to help. I'm going to delve into those areas that I've seen wreak the most havoc.

The Problem of Control

If you set up a trust to direct your child to a certain profession, to take over the family business, to adopt a certain religious belief, or to control whom they will marry, you're trying to control their life from the grave. These types of controls more often than not fail. Children generally have their own ambitions and ideas for their future. Their actions do not always coincide with what we would have them do or with the wisdom that we wish to impart about their chosen path. For example, a trust restriction that provides for the education of a child only if they become a teacher may compel that child to get a teaching credential and to teach one or two years but then reject teaching as a profession after the controls have been lifted. The same can be said for providing benefits only if the child attends a certain religious seminary or marries a certain person. These types of restrictions tend only to frustrate the beneficiary and generate hatred and bitterness against the person imposing the constraint.

While we may see the path our children choose as fruitless, I believe it is far more important to support them in whatever choices they make in a constructive way. Instead of just giving them money, insist they must be able to get a job and support themselves with the choices they make; it will engender more rational thought about their own survival.

I have found that the better provisions in a trust grant choices to the beneficiary within certain boundaries. The goal should be to promote the development of a productive, self-sustaining individual who contributes to himself and society. Efforts to control behavior or choices of our children should be viewed from a greater perspective of wanting our children to be happy and self-sufficient rather than having them emulate what we want.

Caring for Yourself: Problems with the Grantor Trust or Living Trust

In the first chapter, I talked briefly about a living trust. We tend to create these trusts believing them to be the vehicle that allows us to be the first trustee and to handle our affairs as if we still owned them. It is a revocable trust, but one of the common misconceptions is that even though our assets are in trust, we still own them. The fact is in a revocable living trust, we do not legally own the assets because we have transferred title of the assets into the trust. But since we are the first trustees, we can operate as if we still own all the assets because we have the power to revoke the trust, and we have named ourselves as the first trustee. The living trust is an important vehicle for transitioning from life through last illness to death and then to transfer the assets to our named trustee. Problems arise with the living trust, however, when we omit the most important part of this trust.

A living trust allows us to spell out how we expect to be cared for in our final years and what decisions should be made on our behalf. While we may not like to confront this fact, the reality is that we are living longer and living often with a disability requiring personal assistance and care. If you have not established a plan for your own care, you may be the first victim of your own lack of a proper estate plan. It is vital that you talk openly with your lawyer about what could happen and how you want your affairs to be handled. Sadly many elderly are left to the care of strangers as families are too busy to take care of their own. Sometimes, even when they are in the care of family, (because they haven't left a thorough inventory), their assets, jewelry, and even property tend to disappear at the hands of those who have been hired and have no stake in their care and see these- possessions as unattended and vulnerable.

Do our caregivers know how we want our records kept, how we want to live, including our day-to-day care and activities? Have we spelled out where we want to be in this eventuality? Do not abdicate decision making to others. Take the time to plan for your own infirmity! It is usually at this stage of our lives that things go awry. Certain caretakers take advantage of their elderly patients, and the elder is so scared to be left alone that they sign over what they have to assure continuity. What's perhaps even worse is when the elderly, with the onset of dementia, turn on the family member who cares for them. Alzheimer's, in particular, is a particularly debilitating disease where the person often turns on their caregivers, family, and friends or lapses into delusional fantasies. Most family members distance themselves from the erasable relative and the relative is left with strangers.

Our sense of responsibility for our loved ones has diminished over my lifetime, as I see fewer and fewer families willing to take on the burden of care for their infirm family members. It is a time when we focus on ourselves and our own needs and often forget or ignore the needs of those around us. Whether our children will care for us or not is pure speculation. For this reason, planning for our own care and maintenance becomes essential.

Bloodlines

There was a time when leaving everything to the spouse automatically meant those assets would go to your children and then to your grandchildren. Not so anymore. I often hear from parents who are concerned the son-in-law will wind up with the money they leave to their daughter and then leave it to his second wife rather than to their grandchildren. The daughter may also leave her inheritance by will or gift to her spouse only to find that her spouse divorces her and she is left with nothing. In any of these instances, your grandchildren are not guaranteed to receive the benefits you may have intended for them.

The concern is a real one as the laws are geared to favor the spouse because the presumption is that spouses love and care for one another and would not take advantage of the other. There is also a presumption that parents take care of their children. Our laws, in fact, are based on many assumptions that people will honor their family and commitment to each other.

As sad as it may sound, circumstances and feelings change. Life is not always kind, and perspectives change with different life experiences. As well as you think you know someone, situations may arise that surprise you as to reactions, thought processes, or actions. You may trust this person implicitly; nonetheless, it is always better to set things up so you don't have to trust. Remember, the divorce rate is now at around 50 percent and most of those marriages swore to be together until death.

In most states in the United States, gifts and inheritances belong solely to the person named as the beneficiary. If the person receiving the gift or inheritance keeps those assets in their name separate and apart from the ownership of others, it often will remain their property. However, if the person who receives the gift or inheritance shares it with another by placing it in a joint account or giving it to another, he or she may lose possession of the gift or inheritance.

The fact that a child may give their inheritance away to their spouse or others often creates a dilemma for the parent. Fearing that the gift or inheritance will be given away by their child, parents put into place things like life interests or create a trust to assure that their assets wind up in the hands of their grandchildren. The problem with all of this is that while it is important that the assets ultimately go to the grandchildren, they do not like to tie the hands of their children by forming a trust with someone else in charge of family money. So what to do?

One compromise is to create a life interest in the trust for your child with your child as trustee and your grandchildren the beneficiary of the trust. Your child is granted authority to invade the trust and use the assets, but must report and account to the ultimate beneficiary of the trust, the grandchildren. Such a trust does not preclude the child from invading the trust assets, but with the requirement of accounting and reporting to the grandchildren about what they did with the money or assets, it is less likely that all the assets will be dissipated. Safeguards should be established in the trust regarding invasion of principle and required accountings and reports to assure that assets are not squandered.

Economic Constraints – The Problem of "Pot" Trusts

Many trusts are created that establish a fund in which the beneficiaries have an undivided share. The percentage interest of the whole may be set forth, but the assets are either not readily divisible, or the trust was intended as a pot or chest of funds subject to the discretionary distributions of the trustee. But what happens when the trust pot does not have enough to go around or when one beneficiary uses up more than his/her share?

I have seen much grief over these so-called "pot trusts." Perhaps the trustee acquiesced to a distribution to one beneficiary for attending a private East-Coast school at the level of $52,000 a year in tuition, plus room and board, but there are four beneficiaries of the trust and only $600,000 in the trust. The kid who wants the private education is taking more than his share, but if there is no language enforcing equal shares, legally the trustee can grant that distribution. Now you would think this kind of distribution would be a breach of the trustee's duty not to favor one beneficiary over another, yet many trusts grant discretionary authority to the trustee, allowing for this kind of result.

A dissipation of the funds for one beneficiary at the expense of the others *can* leave the trustee exposed to a claim for a breach of fiduciary duty, but it also has an equally bad outcome: the beneficiaries are at each other's throats.

The only reasonable solution to the problems of a pot trust is to divide the assets in equal shares at the beginning of the trust. Then special needs of the individual beneficiary will not impact the proportionate share of another beneficiary, only that beneficiary's proportionate share. This also avoids liability by the trustee who can defend his/her/its decisions by attributing the assets proportionately.

Avoid the Pitfalls of Family and Personal Issues

Though many estate plans go awry, there are some that work. While I have not conducted a scientific survey, by my own observations, the plans that tend to work best are those where there are no controversies, hidden jealousies, or bad feelings toward one another. The family that unites at death also unites to solve the estate issues. Also where there is an only child and he/she gets the entire estate on death, controversy is eliminated.

However, most of us do not have the perfect family and are subject to the issues that cause difficulties after death: 1) multiple marriage families usually involving divorce; 2) sibling rivalries; 3) family member rivalries and jealousies; 4) trusts that last for several generations; 5) bad feelings of the grantor toward any group or relative; 6) uneven distributions; 7) poor trustee performance and management; 8) poor planning for assets and distribution; and 9) ambiguities in the trust. Again, not all estate plans fail, but if you don't have "the perfect family" when you're creating your estate plan, you need to plan better. You know what problems beset your family. In order to keep any kind of family harmony, you must anticipate what will happen based on that knowledge. You can't plan for everything, but you can look into the future based on the past, and that's the best insurance you have when you're planning your estate. We have to start placing ourselves and our decisions in the real word.

Language Problems

I've just outlined some of the more egregious areas that create problems in trusts; however, if I had to name the number-one problem with trusts as they are created today, I would say that unclear, convoluted language is it. The problems with language start because the estate planner doesn't use specific language to personalize your trust. Even though he's listening intently to you as you talk about yourself and your assets, he's thinking about taxes and of the kind of trust you need. He's also mentally sifting through the various form language he should use.

Most people don't know it, but estate lawyers use something called "form books" that contain form language, literally, language that is already written that can cover a variety of situations. (One common form book in use is the Knowles Publishing Estate Planning Series.) The language in the form books comes from case law, history, and statute. The estate lawyer structures this form language around the basic information you give to him. Because there is no design for trusts that is standard in the industry, the lawyer rarely maps out a plan for your trust. So there are often inconsistent directives and even contradictory language. I recently saw one trust that used five different terms for the same person!

You ask, how can this be? Well, the first problem with language is the generic terms like "welfare" and "support" that are so commonly incorporated in our trust and estate documents today. Rarely do these terms have definitions and hence values attached to them. The terms are instead left to the discretion and good graces of the person we appoint as our personal representative. This is a mistake. The broader the term, the greater the leeway in its definition and the more likely the term will be misinterpreted, not followed, or abused.

To show you what I mean, the following paragraph is an example of a trust with undefined terms. I found it under the trust purpose paragraph in a case I was working on early in my career:

> *The purpose of this trust is to provide a vehicle for the orderly management and investment of Settlor's [the grantor's] assets during their lifetimes and the efficient disposition of such assets at their deaths, and to provide for the financial security and general welfare of Settlors and their family.*

If you had to read it a few times to begin to understand what it is saying, you're not alone. But even if you did understand it, don't get complacent that you know what's going on because the next sentence in the trust compounds the mushy language of the first paragraph with more ambiguity:

> *The trustee shall distribute such amounts of income or principal or both…as is necessary for the health, education, maintenance and support of the surviving spouse.*

Now you may be thinking, what's the problem with that? Here's the rub: do the terms "financial security" and "maintenance and support" mean the same thing? What does "general welfare" mean? When I first read this, I kept hoping the terms would be defined in the trust document somewhere but, alas, they were not. I then thought, "Surely the definitions must be established in the statutes or in case law." Unfortunately, this also was not the case.

When asked to rule on trusts, the courts have interpreted certain provisions of specific trust instruments, but the ruling may or may not be a precedent in the next case. The court's rulings tend to be case specific and provide little guidance in the interpretation of provisions for any other trust or in any standard manner. The problem with the above trust paragraph is the terms were not defined, no set boundaries could be made for the decision-making process. And because the terms were not defined, when the trustee interpreted the terms in a way that the beneficiaries didn't like, the beneficiaries didn't have a legal leg to stand on. With language like this, whatever the trustee decided to do was pretty much what happened.

While the trust document may appear neutral on its surface, hidden in the mix are those time bombs I keep talking about. Language like the following is typical of complex trusts that are expected to last for generations:

> *All of the aforesaid real and personal property to be held in trust for the purpose of securing to (wife) and (children) of (grantor) the benefit and enjoyment of the net rents, issues and profits of this trust ... Upon the death of either of the beneficiaries last mentioned, the money which would have been paid to such deceased beneficiary if living shall be paid to and divided among the descendants of such deceased beneficiary.*

Innocently, it appears the grantor is taking care to assure that his/her lineal descendants will be benefited by his money and assets. Unfortunately, in this instance the grantor had two wives. He was married to the second wife only for six months, but she had a child. The grantor died before he could clarify his wishes, and the stage was set for litigation between the two wives, children, and grandchildren who were all claiming rights to his estate. The children and grandchildren were the ultimate losers because the litigation costs consumed much of the estate with the remaining portion divided evenly between the two. As I pointed out in the previous section, the grantor could have solved this problem in the beginning with better planning.

Right now the best way to prevent a nasty scenario from taking place is to attach clear letters of instruction to your trust. They should be written to help guide your executors and trustees in decisions regarding estate and trust matters. The trustee or executor is in a no-win situation. They assume the liability for all the assets under their control and must account to the beneficiaries for their actions and decisions. If they guess wrong, they assume liability for the wrong decision.

When I read through trusts and estates, I often find that the grantor, probably unknowingly, has relieved their trustee or representative of liability for their negligence, relieved them of their obligation to report and account, or granted broad powers to use trust or estate assets as they see fit. These latter kinds of clauses especially make me cringe. For example,

The trustee shall act according to their best judgment and discretion and they shall not be held liable for any errors of judgment or discretion and no trustee shall be liable for the acts or omissions of any other trustee, and no trustee shall incur any personal liability on account of anything that it or he may do or omit to do under the provisions of this deed, except in case of its or his gross negligence or misconduct...

or

No Trustee shall incur any personal liability on account of anything that it may do or omit to do under the provisions hereof, except in cases of its gross negligence or misconduct.

Basically, these clauses allow the trustee or representative to take your money, dispose of it in ways the beneficiaries could never imagine, and ignore with impunity their obligations as trustee. If you have any type of clause like this in your trust, *get rid of it*. If you don't know it now, your beneficiaries will find out later how the language of their trust caused them to lose their inheritance.

These and clauses like them grant to the personal representative the ability to sidestep duties. They give the trustee too much power to do as they want rather than as directed by the trust instrument and too much discretion to defend a wrong decision. In other words, the above language allows your trustee far too much leeway to interpret things the way they want rather than following the directives we give.

Here's another typical clause:

The Trustee shall have the power to use and apply such part or all of the principal of the Trust as the Trustee, in the Trustee's discretion, deems necessary for the health, support, maintenance and education of the surviving Trustor and the issue of Trustor taking into consideration, to the extent the Trustee deems advisable any independent income or other resources of the surviving Trustor or of such issue outside of the Trust and known to the Trustee including but not limited to the assets and income of the beneficiary.

To be fair, the intent of such a provision most likely is to allow the trustee to determine independently the needs of the beneficiaries and to not deplete the funds unnecessarily where the beneficiary should be using their own funds instead of those of the trust. That funds will not simply be depleted and will be there when needed is, of course, a reasonable concern of the grantor. But a breakdown of the clause reveals areas that can be interpreted in a manner different from what the grantor intends.

Assume for a moment that the father (the grantor) has died and named his son as trustee to care for three beneficiaries: the son, daughter, and the grantor's second wife. The second wife is in her seventies and needs the income from the trust to survive. However, the two children from the first marriage are the ultimate remainder beneficiaries of any proceeds left when the second wife dies. This creates an immediate conflict of interest because the children of the first marriage have an interest in the funds that is adverse to the second wife's interest. The assets will be depleted by the second wife's need for support, yet a preservation of those same funds would ultimately benefit the children of the first marriage. Furthermore, while the grantor has created conditions for the spouse to invade principal, she has to jump over almost-impossible hurdles to do so. The first hurdle for the surviving spouse to obtain trust funds is to convince the trustee, her stepson, that the funds will be used by her for the purpose of her "health, support, maintenance and education." Once the spouse has satisfied the first condition, she must convince her stepson that she does not have sufficient income or other outside resources with which to meet her request. In these types of situations, I have seen trustees demand financial statements, tax returns for three years, evidence of all means of support, and a list of assets owned by the beneficiary. In short, in order to get any money from the trust, the spouse must submit to an absolute invasion of privacy in order to meet next-to-impossible standards. Since the ultimate decision maker, the stepson trustee, can make it as difficult or as easy as he wants for the second spouse, it is not hard to see that the second wife may receive little or nothing in distributions.

Furthermore, the conditions for obtaining the benefits are so vaguely worded that if the trustee chooses for any reason to deny the request, the spouse will simply be out-of-luck. There is no real ability to challenge the trustee's denial because such broad discretion has been granted in the trust. This is where the breakdown occurs. The trustee may simply respond that the beneficiary must utilize any other assets she has to meet her own needs rather than invade the trust. As arbitrary as this decision may sound, because of the vague language, a challenge against it usually will not succeed.

Language about Goals

The other area that is open to language abuse is under the goals section of the trust. You know from part one that you must clearly define your goals so that those involved with the trust have a clear map to follow. However, the purpose of a trust is often defined in broad terms like the following:

> *The purpose of this trust is to provide for my and my spouse's care support and maintenance for life and to fully settle our estates upon our death precluding to the greatest extend the need for any court supervision.*

You should now recognize that the terms "maintenance for life" and "care and support" are undefined terms. However, there is another less-apparent problem with this example. This type of language is usually seen in living trusts where the grantor serves as the first trustee and he/she wants the latitude to do with his/her assets as he/she pleases. But because there are no directions that specify otherwise, this same language will apply to the successor trustee when the grantor dies or suffers incapacity. For example, what if a corporate trustee, such as a bank, steps in as successor? How will this language be interpreted? If the purpose of your trust is not defined, and the parameters for the exercise of powers is open-ended, you set your trust up for loss. So too, without a plan in place the grantor's goals will most likely be supplanted by the goals and wishes of the administrator.

Finally, there is one other very dangerous clause in this language: *"precluding to the greatest extent the need for any court supervision."* This most likely was intended by the grantor to avoid the cost associated with court supervision, but this language actually removes the safeguard of oversight by the court. This means the trustee acts with impunity, with no supervision, and will self-validate his/her own decisions.

Where the language is not specific, interpretation of the document is left to whom we place in charge. After all it is their interpretation of the document that governs, so what does it mean to "ensure the health education and welfare of my spouse and children"? Answer: it means whatever the trustee says it means. If the trustee interprets the term "education" to mean four years of college only, then that is what will be enforced. If the child needs a fifth year to graduate, the trustee in the exercise of his or her discretion can deny that fifth year. Would the grantor have made a different decision? Would the grantor have authorized room and board fees, book fees, tutors, and possible travel as a part of the education component of his or her trust? Not surprisingly, we usually never know because the grantor is usually no longer around to tell us. It is the administrator who decides the fate of our children, our spouse(s), and our assets, not us.

What it always comes down to is this: goals should be set forth in detail with benchmarks established to measure performance. If the trust's goal is not accomplished within a certain period of time, the trust should specifically spell out that it either must be terminated and assets distributed or the trustee removed in favor of a better performing representative. Long-term trusts, of course, can and should be established to provide for a disabled person, minor, elderly person, charity, mentally impaired individual, or other legitimate cause. Yet in each of these instances there is a predictable end to services and benefits. Instead of relying on general, vague language, each situation should be analyzed for the logical end-date of benefits and the ultimate distribution defined and specifically stated in the trust.

The Broad Grant of Discretionary Authority

Perhaps the most egregious of all language problems in a trust come with the language that grants broad authority to the trustee. This is the language that the woman with whom I opened this chapter was very concerned about, as the grant of broad authority was exactly what the bank was asking the woman and her husband to sign. Most estate planners are aware they cannot anticipate all the contingencies that may occur in any estate plan. So instead of trying to anticipate events, they usually try to protect the estate by granting broad powers to the trustee, so the trustee can accommodate to changing issues and times. There is a presumption made that the trustee will do the right thing, act in the interest of the beneficiaries alone, and act within legal parameters. When this assumption proves wrong the trust and estate are vulnerable to abuse and loss.

While the estate planners include broad powers to make their jobs easier, professional fiduciaries are more insidious. They frequently count on the broad grant of powers in the trust because it allows them broad authority to do practically anything they like with the funds and assets they manage. The broad grant of powers allows them to establish their own standards and rules of performance. Here's an example of this kind of language:

> *In addition to the powers granted to the trustees in other sections of this trust, the trustee shall have the power to invest in any type of investment. No category or type of investment shall be prohibited and the universe of investments is not limited in any way other than as dictated by the trustees' exercise of reasonable care.*

Once I point this out to people, common sense tells them that such broad language gives their representatives too much power. I was recently involved in a breach of fiduciary case in which language similar to the above was interpreted by the professional trustee to allow investment in real property. The fiduciary invested the $1.8 million held in the trust in two properties valued at close to $5 million. But the investment did nothing for the trust except encumber it with a $3.2 million debt, and any income from the property was consumed by servicing the debt and the fiduciary's administrative fees. On the other hand, it more than doubled the value of assets under management for the professional trustee that charged fees at the rate of far more than the 2.5 percent of the value of assets. In addition, the trustee charged a real property management fee of 4 percent of the gross income of the property. In other words, the income was consumed with management fees and servicing the $3.2 million debt; there was nothing left for the income beneficiaries. Was this legal? Yes, it was. Is this what the grantor intended? Probably not.

If you already have a will or a trust, pull it out and look at this section, and see how much discretionary power you are granting to your personal representative. Read it carefully, and you will be amazed at the unfettered, unsupervised, extensive authority you grant to them over all that is dear to you.

The final and perhaps most egregious problem that arises out of a broad grant of powers is that with it, investment powers are often even broader that the general powers of the trustee. The Knowles Publishing Estate Planning Series offers up some very disturbing language:

> *Investments may be held and acquired without any limitation or standard that (1) requires diversification of investment and risk of investment, including investments involving a prudent speculation that the value of an investment or a cash flow from an investment will increase over them; (2) precludes a trust from participating in closely held business [a nonpublic corporation that is owned by a small number of shareholders where stock is publicly traded but most is held by a few shareholders who have no plans to sell] and investment ventures and in acquiring an ownership position in a company, partnership, or other venture that is not registered for sale to the general public and that is subject to contractual restrictions that limit the marketability and transferability of an equity interest; or (3) limits the authority of a trustee to acquire, hold or own non-income producing property."*

Basically, if you sign something like this, you are allowing your trustee to do whatever they want with your funds. This is exactly the kind of clause that was used in the couple who lost everything when their lawyer became their trustee. Again, to be fair, this broad grant of investment authority was intended no doubt to give the personal representative latitude to make appropriate decisions for the family, and the language will vary from estate planner to estate planner. But no matter what the variation, the language can be interpreted to mean that investments may be held indefinitely or continually churned and anywhere in between. Again we rely upon the integrity of our trustee to do the right thing.

Whether the trustee performs in a manner consistent with our wishes depends in large part upon how well we planned. It is unfair to leave the trustee in the dark and with no clear direction, which is exactly what we do when we include broad, vague language. In essence, with this language, you have abdicated to the trustee decisions that you should have made for yourself and your family. What is interesting is that most lay and professional trustees alike have a love/hate relationship with the trust because of these very provisions. Professional fiduciaries often complain that they dislike trust and estate management because of the time involved and ambiguities in the documents. They find that the instruments prepared are often inconsistent in terms and obligations making their job unwieldy. So while the broad grant of powers was originally designed to alleviate these types of problems, they actually make them worse.

But who is watching the store? Rarely does a trust include directions to account for the decisions made in the name of the trust. Rarely are checks and balances put in place to assure the decisions made are indeed on behalf of our beneficiaries and not to the benefit of the trustee who manages the funds. Typical discretionary language may appear as follows:

> *Powers of the Trustee: To carry out the purposes of any trust created under this instrument... The trustee may apply to the benefit of the beneficiary as much of the beneficiary's trust as the Trustee, in the trustees discretion deems necessary for the beneficiary's proper support, health, maintenance and education...*

More and more I have been seeing language in our trusts and estates that are not defined, allowing variation from trust officer to trust officer or estate planner to estate planner. Because there is no standard against which definitions and performance are measured, we have left our beneficiaries at the mercy of the people we leave in charge. However well intentioned our fiduciaries may be, it is simply not acceptable that the playing field can be shifted and manipulated to suit the needs, desires, and machinations of a poorly performing or dishonest fiduciary at the expense of our beneficiaries.

The Fiduciary Industry

The trust and estate industry is an industry based on history, premised on years of estate law and precedent derived from English feudal law. (That's law that was on the books in 1066—over a thousand years ago!) It is an industry that fails to connect the dots from the estate plan to the administrative plan and hence creates a system that frustrates almost everyone who deals with it. There is much blame to go around as the people who administer the plans are often burdened with years of history not only in the law but in the families themselves, which also colors how the plan will actually play out.

Our trust in a system that is trustworthy implies there are parameters and safeguards to catch the people we place in positions of trust when they err. Unfortunately the safeguards are usually too costly to enforce, so the problems go unaddressed. Because I have handled all sides of an estate plan, I can tell you that many trusts do not play out as anticipated. Many fail to address the myriad of issues that relate to the estate and families they touch and sadly create controversy and problems that could have been avoided. There are many factors that make the will or trust subject to controversy that have nothing to do with the estate planner, such as the personalities of the family involved; the person chosen as the administrator; the disputes over family property and its division; the rivalries and bad blood that existed before the death of the grantor; resentment in the family for disproportionate responsibility for elder care or family issues; and of course my all time favorite—the grantor's failure to address issues out of spite or ignorance, intentionally leaving his or her heirs to battle it out and clean up the mess. The sad part is, through all of it, the only winners tend to be the lawyers and professionals who are brought in at the trust's expense to deal with the problems that have been created.

CHAPTER FIVE

The Tradition of Trust—Whom do you trust?

It should be clear to you by now that the way trusts are currently written leaves the beneficiaries relatively powerless against the trust's appointed representatives. But the fact remains, once you name them, these representatives are your trustees. They are the people you place in charge of handling your money, your assets and your family when you're gone. You want to believe they are going to do their utmost to ensure your trust is handled with care and honesty. You trust that they are going to carry out your wishes with all due care.

It is no easy task deciding who will represent you and your interests when you're gone. There are some very good, conscientious trustees out there doing the job that has been asked of them, but the sad truth is, many of those involved with your trust have figured out how to rip you off—it is a trillion dollar industry, after all. This chapter delves into the issues surrounding a trustee, from the best type of trustee to choose, to the sometimes overwhelming problems a trustee faces when he/she/it isn't given clear direction in the trust. I also give you a peek into some of the abuses I have seen on the part of the trustee—some intentional and some not. To err is human, certainly, but I often wonder where is the line drawn between a trustee unintentionally making a decision that benefits him or her, to behavior that can only be construed as self-serving and even fraudulent?

Who Will Represent You?

> *I have five or six friends that I can think of right now who would step in to administer my estate for me if I died. They are smart enough that they could figure out what they had to do. I do not consider this a problem.*

A young father, divorced, Silicon Valley executive said this to me at a dinner party when I described in detail the process that I was going through to develop a trustworthy system for the administration of trusts.

It struck me that there is a real perception, particularly among younger people, that they have friends, colleagues, or family members who would step forward to take care of their assets and families in the event that something happened to them. They also believe that they would step forward to help out a friend if that friend died. And make no mistake, many would do it selflessly. Yet most of these friends are clueless as to the exact responsibility they are assuming by assenting to being administrator of a trust. So noble as this young man's sentiments may be, his statement is really based on ignorance of what really is involved in handling another person's estate or trust. Sure they want to help, but do they have any training to do the job? What about the responsibility and the time commitment that goes with the job, not to mention the self-sacrifice, if the person is not even paid. What about the liability if mistakes are made? Will the beneficiaries of the estate or trust be as forgiving as the deceased friend might be if errors are made?

My former husband was a middle-aged lawyer in a small firm when he died. He thought he had friends in his firm. He had practiced with these individuals for twenty years and thought he could count on them. He named his law partners specializing in tax and estate planning to serve as executor of his estate. Certainly not thinking he would die at so young an age, he named two lawyers he worked with as his personal representative. He was sure they would assist his family if he died. He thought who better to serve than someone in the field? But when he suffered a brain aneurysm at age fifty and when it came time for these individuals to step forward to serve as the personal representative of his estate, each declined in sequence.

While this may not be the scenario that plays out in all cases, my experience has shown me that what you expect to happen frequently does not happen. The general perception is that all we have to do is name a representative, they will serve, and it will work as we have planned. This, in large part, is a myth. If you have named a personal representative and not a bank, these people often consider it their duty or obligation to help in a time of crisis, feel compelled to act, and so are snared into the fiduciary role. Still others covet these positions motivated by a desire to control family wealth. Many decline if they have nothing to gain from such appointment, as it involves a lot of work, responsibility, and exposure to liability for mistakes. If you name a personal friend or family member to represent you and your estate, it may cost you less in fees, but the person you have chosen frequently has no training in trust or estate administration, and this, in itself, can become a very costly problem.

Duties of the trustee are extensive and liability associated with the role can be daunting. But if you decide to go the other route and name a professional fiduciary, you run other types of risks from having your trust drained by fees and even bad investments to self dealing by your fiduciary, indifference to your beneficiaries and negligence in the handling of your assets.

Naming a trustee is one of the most important decisions you can make as you go through the process of creating your trust. However, the current practice is to simply abdicate authority to someone, either a personal representative or professional fiduciary, for the decisions that we are not there to make. The current system is all premised on the belief that we can do nothing else. Those who create and oversee estates want us to believe that since we are no longer around, we should simply trust the system to work. But while this is the prevailing belief, the system is outdated. You can trust your trustee if—and only if—you can trust the trust instrument itself.

Whom Can You Trust?

> *Trust but verify.*
> —Ronald Reagan

When you think about whom you want to represent you in your trust, you want someone you can trust to take care of you, your spouse, and your children when you are ill, elderly, or no longer around. You want to be certain that they will decide questions about your family and your money the way you would, and you really want to believe that they, without question, will carry out your wishes if you are not there to direct them. They will always be there as your family and children age and will take care of them as you would. The only way to ensure any of the above will be true is to really think about situations that may exist when we die.

Because trusts are so poorly designed and directions for implementation are practically non-existent, we leave a vacuum of information that we expect our personal representatives to answer for us. Yet our personal or professional trustees are often in the dark as to how we would handle certain situations or how we would decide issues. With this lack of direction and information, who can blame them if they impose their own wishes on the trust rather than ours?

I can't sugarcoat this one. With the system as it currently stands, none of your choices for personal representative can truly earn the trust that most estate plans demand of them. Personal trustees seldom have the experience to manage a trust and certainly don't offer accountability, and professional trustees have inherent conflicts, lack of time, and other weaknesses.

So what do you do? The simple answer is that you write a better trust, one that includes a plan with your goals and values clearly stated and your implementation strategies well thought out. You can trust someone to act on your behalf if they know what to do, have clear direction, and are accountable to more than just themselves. But while we may know the first trustee we list in our trust, and they may serve with integrity and conscientiousness, it is the person we do not know well or at all that will succeed them and who may compromise our goals and wishes. We should plan for the fact that strangers will be administering our estate or trust, someone we have never met, who knows nothing about us and doesn't care. If we view our estate plan from this perspective, we will plan better, provide a clear implementation and execution plan, and be forced to deal with issues we have traditionally abdicated to others to solve for us.

The Problematic Role of Parent

To better equip you to accomplish all I just mentioned, it is vital that you understand the various roles a trustee plays and the problems inherent in those roles. But what job does a trustee do? Is trust administration, the job of a trustee, just another financial service? For those who do this job, they will respond with a resounding "no." To be a trust officer you must be a financial advisor, accountant, psychologist, mentor, caregiver, investor, teacher, in short a parent, asset manager, and investment manager. All three overlap in the trustee context, but this division of roles has, so far, gone unrecognized and that has caused all sorts of problems. While the asset manager and investment manager roles are well known, and may even be familiar territory for a financial institution, the role of parent is not. The "parental" role is the distinguishing feature between trust administration and other financial services banks offer; however, if one of the three roles is ignored by the trustee, he or she can veer off course.

After years of research into what goes wrong with trusts, I have concluded that the failure to recognize the full-parental role of the trustee is a major stumbling block in the development of adequate trust models.

While the grantor is alive, the trustee can confer with and rely on him or her to direct the decisions of the trust, but once the grantor dies and the administrator takes charge of the irrevocable trust, too little attention is given to the parental shoes in which the trustee is placed. Because there is so little guidance in the implementation aspect of setting up a trust, and the language is often so vague, no direction is given to the trustee as to how he/she/it is to fulfill the role of parent.

Is the Bank a Good Parent?

Banks took over the handling of trusts as professional fiduciaries because they saw it as a way to offer personalized service to their very wealthy clients and in turn, they hoped they would receive lucrative commercial business from those clients. Since trusts have become more and more mainstream, banks are inundated with trusts. They have thousands of trusts sitting in files, and the only ones that receive individual attention—no matter how much the banks protest and promise otherwise—are those that are very complex and have assets over $5 million. So with an average of one hundred to one hundred and fifty trusts per trust officer at major banks, and tens of thousands under management each trust isn't going to receive personalized attention. To handle the huge amounts of trusts it carries, banks have spent their time focusing on their administration as investor and asset manager. In this regard, they have implemented checks and balances to monitor what they can measure, but what the banks have not addressed is their interaction between parental role, asset manager, and investor. Just to give you an idea of the complexity of this problem, the following lists the broad categories of people to whom the trust officer serves as parent:

- **Adult Beneficiaries.** A trustee is most often a surrogate for the grantor who is usually the parent, grandparent, or other elder relative of the beneficiaries. By virtue of the relationship between a beneficiary and the grantor, the latter carries what is called "social authority." In other words, because it's the grantor's money, even when it is in a trust, he or she still has a natural authority over the decisions being made. So while the grantor still lives, the trustee acts within the mantel of this social authority. However, when the grantor dies, the social authority associated with the grantor disappears, but the trustee must still make parental-type decisions. While the grantor was alive, this wasn't an issue, but once the grantor is gone, the adult beneficiaries view this as the trustee exercising control over their lives, and they no longer psychologically view that control as legitimate. Without the mantel of social authority, the legal power the trustee exercises over the trust engenders resentment and even distrust on the part of the adult beneficiaries.

- **Aging Beneficiaries.** More and more trustees are becoming custodians of elderly people often confined to a care facility in their final years. If the trust is a living trust, this may be the grantor him/herself who now depends upon the named trustee to oversee his/her care and make decisions regarding finances, investments, bill paying, maintenance, housing, medical care, nutrition, and social activities not to mention interaction with other family members. These are not traditional roles of our financial institutions. When we start to lose our ability to care for ourselves and, frankly, to protect what we have, even if we are still alive, those we have put in charge have access to everything we have. We may be completely dependent upon a financial institution to oversee our own care, our finances, etc. Do you want your bank deciding where to put you when you cannot speak for yourself? They may act on our behalf, in our interest or not, and there is really no one to assure they are making decisions that are truly best for us. Since we are still alive, there is little to no oversight of our fiduciaries. Remember, no oversight means power to do as he or she chooses. Think about it. If you have left a bank in charge of you, how much nurturing, care, and protection do you really think you will get?

- **Minor Beneficiaries.** The role of a trustee as custodian to minor beneficiaries is truly placing the trustee in the role of parent. In this regard, the trustee may be required to oversee the parental care of a minor beneficiary and may be forced to interact with surrogate parents who 1) may resent having to apply for funds from the trust for the care of minor relatives for whom they have assumed responsibility or 2) are interested in gaining access to the benefits of the trust and not necessarily applying those benefits for the care of the minor child. In other instances, the trustee may be placed in the untenable position of overseeing the trust for multiple generations, weighing the interests of each against available assets.

- **Disabled Beneficiaries.** For the disabled beneficiary, either a minor or an adult, the trustee may be in charge of personal injury funds or family funds set up to care for the individual. Our trustees are expected to make decisions regarding everything from general expenses to housing, support, education, transportation, maintenance, and the general welfare of the recipient beneficiary. By definition, these decisions are placing the trustee in the role of parent. But if the trustee is a professional fiduciary, this creates huge headaches because our financial institutions are not trained to be parents.

The Liabilities of Being a Parent

As you can imagine, most trustees and, most especially, professional fiduciaries do not function well in the role of parent—nor do they like this role. They are neither trained nor do they possess the tools to function in this capacity. Yet they are often thrust in this role as the sole trustee. More often than not, they do not have answers to family situations because the grantor did not provide guidance. As the appointed trustee, the professional fiduciary with no clear guidance will make decisions such as whether the assets you have left in trust will allow your children to go to graduate school. He or she will also make discretionary decisions like where they will go or what the trust will pay for, and the fiduciary will ultimately decide whether trust assets may be used by your beneficiaries to start a business or whether buying a home or renting an apartment fits in the definition of "general welfare" as it is defined by your trust. The professional fiduciary also decides when distributions are to be made, in what amounts, and to whom.

It is the parental role we impose on our representatives, both personal and professional, that often sets them up for liability, dispute, and failure. Who wants to be parented by another when their parents are dead? Who wants to be told by a stranger or others what they can and can't do with their own family money? If the trust names a personal representative, this person often brings to the role all of his or her own experiences, prejudices, family history, and predisposed views on a variety of subjects. Their background is not the same as the grantor's, and their decisions may be very different. In the case of the professional fiduciary, it assigns an individual to interface with the beneficiaries of the trust, but it is largely the views of the institution that will govern the management and disposition of assets. To compound this problem, the views from one trust officer to another may vary, and for large estates where there are multiple beneficiaries and multiple trust representatives, decisions may be inconsistent. For example, two sisters named as beneficiaries of the same trust may live in different locations. The same institutional trustee serves as trustee for both but assigns a local representative to each beneficiary. The different trust representatives may provide conflicting answers to the same inquiry from different beneficiaries.

Decisions regarding education, support, maintenance, necessity of distribution etc. are not investment decisions traditionally made by professional fiduciaries but life decisions. So whether we realize it or not, we expect our trustees to act as sound advisors, not just in the role of how best to invest our money, but how best to raise our children, take care of our spouse, support our disabled child, or fund our businesses. If we expect our representative to serve as a parent, whether that is a personal or professional fiduciary, we must give them clear direction with clear constraints and guidance on how to make decisions for us. These decisions are not easy, and most estate plans simply sidestep them by granting broad authority to the trustee setting up the trust for failure and loss. Instead, we need to address the issues head on. Remember, what you do not decide will be decided for you.

Other Problematic Trustee Roles

The difficulties faced by our trustees are not issues they necessarily anticipate. They may want to do a good job for us but have few tools and little guidance on how to accomplish what we want. Nonetheless, there are certain situations that set our trustees up for failure. We can protect against these, but often we are not aware that we plant the seeds for failure in our trusts early on in the planning stage.

While the parental role a trustee plays definitely represents one of the biggest problems associated with trustees, it is by no means the only one. The following gives three other problematic areas a grantor must be aware of when creating a trust.

Problem Area One: Personal Fiduciary for Life

Usually, trusts designate the named personal representative to serve for *"so long as he/she is able to serve."* This means as long as the personal representative is willing and able to serve or in other words, a lifetime appointment. He or she cannot be removed except for gross negligence. There are pros and cons to such language. If you have the perfect personal representative, you want them to serve as long as they are willing to serve, *but* if the personal representative turns out to be someone who does not get along with the beneficiaries, has less skills than one would have hoped, is preoccupied with duties unrelated to the trust or estate they administer, or worse, is taking trust funds, you would want the person to step aside. But when a representative is named for life—for as long as he or she is able—and this representative does not recognize their limitations or refuses to step aside, the beneficiaries are locked into a course of expensive litigation to get rid of them.

By the way, here is another area where wills and trusts differ. If it is the administration of a will in question, the court may have supervision of the fiduciary, and the beneficiaries can request accountability and/ or removal of the personal representative by the court. There must be a showing of negligence and some egregious conduct, but it is possible with effort to remove the representative. Because there is no formal court supervision with a trust, the beneficiaries have to file a lawsuit to have the trustee removed. This can equate to full litigation against the trustee who will most likely defend his/her/its position at the expense of the trust.

The better-drafted will or trust grants to the beneficiaries the ability to change trustees or personal representatives. While some may argue that this gives the beneficiary the ability to "fiduciary shop," such concerns are usually overstated. Changing fiduciaries does not eliminate the trust or its requirements, but empowers the beneficiaries to find someone with whom they can work and who is willing to do the job. Provisions in the estate or trust plan that allow the personal representative enough protection from disgruntled beneficiaries, while at the same time allowing the beneficiaries to supervise the job performance of their fiduciary with the power to remove them, will go a long way to balancing the interests of the individuals involved in the administrative process.

Problem Area Two: Beneficiary Named as Trustee

A family member who serves as both trustee and beneficiary is placed in a conflict of interest position. Although this is not illegal, the trustee/ beneficiary must take measures to assure that there is no favoring of himself/herself in the decisions made on behalf of the trust or estate. This position in many instances compromises the trustee/beneficiary's own interests *vis-à-vis* the estate or trust as he/she must always act on behalf of the trust or estate over his/her own interests. Those who are not constantly vigilant in promoting the interests of the beneficiaries over their own interests subject themselves to liability. Trustee/beneficiaries often do not recognize the risks inherent in their dual role position and start treating the assets of the trust as their own. This is a mistake.

When planning a trust or estate, consider either appointing siblings jointly as co-trustees or a completely independent party to serve as your personal representative along with the siblings. While I don't think the sibling co-trustee situation is ideal, having a third trustee forces them to cooperate. In other words, the third trustee provides a check and balance to the rivalries of the siblings.

Problem Area Three: A Too-Powerful Trustee

I have already cautioned you at length on the dangers of the broad grant of authority many estate planners put into a trust document, but I want to spend a little time looking at the issue from a trustee perspective. Granting our personal representative broad authority to make decisions on our behalf was always thought to be a way of assuring that they would be able to respond to changing circumstances. While there is wisdom in this thinking, the pendulum has swung too far in favor of complete discretion. Lord Action, the historian, warned that "Power corrupts and absolute power corrupts absolutely." This adage may be applied to our trusts. A grant of absolute authority over our assets and family with locked-in power for life is often simply a license to steal. While one might think the laws will protect our estates and trusts from abuse, it has been my experience that protection is expensive, disruptive, and may consume the very fund it is trying to protect. Our intentions can be subverted because we granted too much authority and that authority is then abused because there is no oversight of our trustees.

Governmental agencies lodged with oversight authority for the professional fiduciary have few tools to monitor the tens of thousands of trusts under management. They do not have the capability of screening trusts for compliance with their provisions, and they do not have the manpower to determine whether the trustee is doing its job. For the personal trustee, there is no oversight of their role as fiduciary at all. Oversight is from the beneficiaries alone.

Despite the best of intentions, it is simply a fact that over time where broad discretionary authority is granted, the intentions of the personal representative supplant the intentions of the grantor. This is true whether it is a personal or professional fiduciary. For example, a sibling trustee who cares for her disabled brother is to receive the assets at his death may make decisions to retain assets rather than spend them on the care for her brother knowing that her share will be greater if the expense is not incurred. From the institutional-trustee perspective, certain fees may be generated for itself in the investment of trust funds in certain property or instruments. If the institutional trustee has a choice to invest in assets that generate an additional fee for itself or an investment that provides no additional fee, the conflict is obvious.

Solution to These Problems:
Protect Your Trustee by Educating Them

To prevent these problems from occurring, it is vital to make sure your goals and values are clearly defined. Only then will the trustee know how you would act in various circumstances. Once that is in place, you must establish safeguards against the trust or estate going off-course. Trust administration is relatively complicated and there are no real courses available to the family trustee on how to administer them. Plan for your representative to retain experts to help him or her, and require annual accountings and reports to the beneficiaries so irregularities can be caught. Set up a screening and prohibitions so conflicts of interest are avoided.

Those who are not familiar with trust administration often invest funds in companies, instruments, real property, etc. in which the trustee holds an interest. This creates a slippery slope as the trust funds become co-mingled with the funds of the trustee. Oftentimes, the decisions concerning investments of a trust's fund are not always consistent with the law, the trust instrument, or even the needs of the beneficiaries because the trustees have no implementation plan to follow.

I have often seen a trustee act as though he or she were some benevolent uncle entitled to get credit for the distributions made. The reality is that the funds in the trust do not belong to the trustee. He/she/it is nothing more than the caretaker for the beneficiaries of their own money. Yet many a trustee deems the funds to be their own. After all, they have power over it. Because of this, the grantor must put in safeguards against the trustee to assure that he/she/it realizes the trust's funds are not available to the trustee for his/her/its own commercial gain.

Empower the beneficiaries to catch conflicts of interest and eliminate them by requiring regular accountings and reports and prohibiting investments that benefit the trustee, not the trust. Above all, authorize your beneficiaries to remove a trustee who fails to honor the directives of the grantor.

Mistakes Made because of Poor Fiduciary Checks and Balances

Trust and Estate Administration is a legal specialty. Errors made in judgment or through naïveté, whether made with the best of intentions or not, can cause significant damage to the estate or trust and loss of assets for the beneficiaries. The mistake may go undetected for years yet causes a ripple effect in the administration as other decisions are based on the original error. This creates a cascading effect that usually culminates in significant loss to the estate or trust.

Choose your representative carefully. Recognize their limitations, and plan to pay for experts to assist them when necessary. Anticipate there will be significant cost in retaining experts to assist the inexperienced fiduciary. But the funds are well worth it as it will avoid a greater loss down the road from poor administration.

What Are My Choices?

Now that you are aware of the different roles and the main problems inherent in those roles, I can help you better understand both the pros and cons of the two main types of trustees. We'll start with the professional fiduciary first.

The Professional Fiduciary

Many select a professional fiduciary to serve as their administrator or trustee because it negates family rivalries. They have investment functions in place, and they are in the business of being a fiduciary. By going this route, you put the trust's assets in the hands of someone trained to do the job. It also solves any succession issues (for example, who's going to take over when your first trustee is gone) that come up with personal representatives because an institution, such as an established bank, should be around for a long time.

The professional fiduciary also has accounting systems in place so it can track the funds, and it has people trained as fiduciaries. But, no surprise, the professional suffers from an inadequate implementation plan for your trust. While the professional fiduciary may have accounting functions in place, they do not do well at guessing what the grantor intended or undertaking the parental role.

Professional fiduciaries also do not have technology that tracks their *decisions*. The professionals have "smart check books," and that is about all. They do not have mechanisms in place to decipher what is meant by the terms of your trust, nor do they have processes or procedures in place to track their decisions so they are consistent from one trust officer to another. Similarly, the professional fiduciary is not able to structure with any consistency how your assets are to be managed, particularly if you have unique assets. The usual response is to sell everything and convert it to cash so it can be put in their money management accounts. Because of this, when you write your trust, require your trustee to prepare a narrative report on the decisions they make on behalf of your trust and beneficiaries annually. Demand that the narrative report explains the decisions behind the numbers. They should be able to explain why one of the trusts assets diminished in value or was sold at a loss, for example. They should explain how they intend to meet the tax liability of the estate with a plan. They should be able to explain why they invested in bank instruments when other investments would have yielded a higher return.

To the professional, being a trustee is a business. It is not a personal favor and it definitely isn't personalized to you for the long term. Once the grantor is dead and the professional fiduciary has control of the assets, the trust model changes to fit the standardized administration model employed by the particular fiduciary. At death when control shifts to the professional, the directives of the grantor are only as good as the trust provides and the beneficiaries enforce.

Another major downfall of this type of fiduciary is that the training of the professional trustee is usually limited to a six- to twelve-week course on fiduciary obligations and regulatory compliance with periodic refresher courses and on-the-job training. It took me many years as a trained attorney in this field to understand the industry, rules, regulations, statutes, obligations, and procedures. The professional fiduciary does not usually have this training and does not hire trained attorneys as trust administrators except when a problem erupts. Often this is too late. So instead of a highly trained individual acting as your trustee and giving you personalized service, you will get a committee to administer your trust with emphasis on preserving assets and generating business for the professional.

The professional also looks at your trust not in terms of how they can help you, but how much risk you represent to them. This is a biggie. From the bank's perspective, the more money in the trust, the more money it will make and the more it is willing to take the risk of the trust's management. The $5 million plus trust allows the bank to hopefully get a better return, and it minimizes its risk of losing money on your money. But the problem here is that while the banks may get a better return, your money may be invested in ways that aren't consistent with your values and may not be getting the return they could get if the full market had been explored. Banks invest in themselves with your money.

Not only are your hard-earned assets and cash not being handled individually as you might think, there's another hidden problem with the bank's lumping funds together. Currently banks do not recognize all the risk they have in the administration of trusts. In the organizational structure of a bank, trusts usually come under the department of asset management, the division that manages money and assets that belong to individuals or institutions. Banks look at your trust in terms of the fees that will be generated from it. If the trust loses money because your trust assets drop in value, the bank doesn't lose any money directly. It may lose it indirectly in the form of reduced-fee income, but that is a minor point to the bank.

If they lose your trust money for you, it doesn't come out of their pocket. It is just too bad for you. Because trusts tend to be "secret" with great emphasis on "private, or confidential services" the losses are usually buried in sterile accountings that never are raised to our attention. Because the beneficiary is usually kept in the dark or fails to notice the losses, it is not until some astute beneficiary actually looks at their trust that the problems are discovered. They also may find these problems too late to recover from the professional. We have been trained to trust our fiduciaries so we don't look closely at trust management. We should

Because we have been complacent and "trusted" the system, all manner of horrible outcomes have befallen our families and our money under the term trust. For our professionals, it is business as usual but it is we who have not been paying attention, mostly because we're not educated on this subject.

Even the professional fiduciary fails to account for its own management of our funds and assets. They do not understand whole areas of trust administration where the risk to their clients places them at risk for lawsuits and liability for losses to their clients. While the bank, in general, has a grasp on ways it can lose money in the form of market risk and credit risk, the risk that actually impacts your trust and the bank that manages it is operational risk.

The Basel Committee on Banking, the guru committee of international banking that meets annually in Basel, Switzerland, defines "operational risk" as "Risk of direct or indirect losses resulting from inadequate or failed internal processes, people and systems or from external events." Mistakes and fraud cost banks because their people and systems are inadequate to handle the task at hand, but the banks aren't aware of the legions of other problems created by the multiple roles they are to play in trust administration, and they fail to capture the risk inherent in each role. Simply put, banks really do not have a handle on the operational risk that can impact whether they do a good job administering your trust or not. Trusts tend to be unique to the individual grantor, beneficiary, and asset mix, but banks have found no formulas or templates to apply to all, or even a few, trusts in their administration. This makes trust risk difficult to actually quantify. As a result, your trust or estate must be handled manually, and to do this, the banks rely on Excel spread sheets and periodic review of the trust instrument for directives. They have recently moved to scanning your trust documents so they do not have to go to the file drawers to re-read the instruments every time, but that is the extent of the technology applied to your trust. Yes, there are sophisticated accounting systems that track the money in and out, but the real analysis of how your trust works is nowhere to be found and that creates a huge amount of risk both for the bank and for your trust.

The problems that arise from no real analysis and mapping of your trust in the first place sets the stage for your plan to go awry. Conclusions reached from reading the language of your trust vary from trust officer to trust officer, and over time consistency suffers. Because the terms used in the trust are not defined, inconsistencies in the terms are not caught and cured before they cause later problems. Standards of performance to meet the grantor's goals are not set, so there is no gauge against which performance can be measured. There is no oversight by an independent entity to assure the trust is complying with the grantor's wishes. And if all that doesn't make you cringe, then remember, the fees charged tend to be significantly greater than represented and change from year to year depending upon current bank policy.

As much as we want to think our financial institutions are looking out after our interests, reality is that the bank looks out for its own interest making your trust profitable for itself. Fees will be extracted from your trust or estate whether it is generating income or growth for the beneficiaries or not. Here a table that lists the pros and cons of naming a professional fiduciary as your trustee:

PROFESSIONAL FIDUCIARY	
Advantages	**Disadvantages**
• This is what they do for a living. • They have investment capability and specialist resources. • Can bundle assets with other trusts to increase return and lower investment risk. • Sophisticated accounting systems. • They will be around from generation to generation.	• Services not personalized; your trust is one of hundreds or thousands. • Administrators may have limited fiduciary training. • Potential conflicts of interest. • Asset-based and transaction-based fees can deplete assets. • Don't perform parental role particularly well. • They never map the trust so it can meet the goals set by the grantor.

When dealing with a professional fiduciary as the trustee or administrator, you as the grantor must recognize what services they can and cannot provide well. The financial institution may direct you to attorneys it designates to draft your will or trust for you, and the attorney will in turn name the financial institution as your fiduciary in the instruments you sign. The language the attorney puts into the documents is, of course, the language the financial institution likes to administer. It may or may not reflect what you really had in mind. And if you do happen to have your own estate planner draft your trust documents, the bank will still want you to sign those dreaded waivers.

It is important that you take responsibility for understanding and knowing what you sign. It will have significant ramifications for you and your heirs. Do not waive your rights to accountings, fiduciary review of prior administration, recovery of assets lost by prior fiduciaries, review and approval of fees charged, fiduciary obligation to pursue claims for the trust, or the right to hold your fiduciary liable for their negligence. It is not in your interest or the interest of your heirs to waive any of these rights.

The Personal Representative: the Relative or Family Friend

We have all heard so many horror stories about the family wealth being dissipated by the professionals that, in droves, we are now naming relatives, children, spouses, best friends, etc. to serve as our trustee. What else are we to do? We want someone who will have our best interests at heart, and we can only hope our family will do the job we are unable to do for ourselves because we are gone. This is the hope phase of trusting our relatives. But remember, we also have the expectation of competence in the people we place in charge.

Sadly, hope and expectations are not enough, and I am not telling you anything new here. However, what is new is saying something about it. Most people hush up on this subject and stick their head in the sand saying, "Well, I trust Uncle Jim (or Uncle Bob or Aunt Mary) to do the best they can." The subject of whom to name as trustee is handled too quickly in resignation because the grantor is under that erroneous notion that they can do nothing else because they will not be around to deal with the issues that arise. (This resigned acceptance of the status quo is the reason I began working with technologists to empower the grantor in estate planning. There was a helplessness that I saw repeatedly with no better answer in sight.)

One of the primary difficulties encountered when naming relatives and friends as trustees and executors is their lack of training for the role they are asked to play. Usually our friends and relatives have a life of their own and are not in training specifically to be ready when the call comes to take over our estate. Nor are they usually interested in serving in this capacity. Sometimes they serve out of a genuine desire to help, but often they serve out of guilt or out of a desire to control the assets among other reasons. Remember the Brooks Astor saga where the son was charged with elder abuse of his own mother because he wanted to transfer to himself over $60 million of his mother's assets while she was ill? Yes, indeed, greed rears its ugly head in these situations all the time.

We want to assume that greed will not motivate our personal representative and that we fall into good hands when we are ill, ailing, demented, or dead. But we can never know if our relatives will protect us or exploit us. I find that if someone was raised as a caring, conscientious, and responsible individual, their children will pick up these values and often will emulate these behaviors. It is not a guarantee, but this is where I see families taking care of one another and trusts working out just fine.

Choosing a family member to represent you based on his or her integrity and willingness to help, however, may not be enough. The lack of training as a trustee or executor can be a significant issue, and I consider it the single greatest detractor of choosing this type of trustee. The personal representative is thrust into all the roles I have already mentioned. I once knew a professor who was named as a trustee of his family's trust, but he felt like an impostor because he lacked knowledge of how to administer the trust or how best to make decisions he was required to make. He simply hoped that because he was not collecting a fee for his services, the beneficiaries would be kind to him if he made mistakes. This is wishful thinking at best. Because any trustee, no matter how intelligent and well meaning, is not the grantor, he or she does not have the grantor's training, history, or experience and, normally will not make decisions like the grantor would.

The people we place in charge of our trusts and estates are often clueless as to their duties, obligations, required performance, and accountability. Not only do they usually know nothing about trust or estate administration, they frequently lack the motivation or opportunity to learn. Where the professional trust officer may have fifty to one hundred or more trusts to manage, the personal fiduciary normally has another life doing something completely different from administering your estate or trust. They may resent the time trust administration takes away from their own life, believe that he/she is doing a favor for the family, and the rules don't apply or my favorite think that the funds are theirs to dole out as they please. Your personal fiduciary may fail to provide regular accountings, fail to properly invest assets, miss deadlines for tax or reporting, and may fail entirely in the fiduciary role. The personal trustee usually has no administrative tools or training and is simply guessing at his or her role as fiduciary. Thus, they operate in unfamiliar territory, make decisions dealing with current needs of the existing beneficiaries, ignoring the risk of the decision to future heirs or different classes of beneficiaries. They fail to account for the trust's assets thinking that family members will forgive these oversights. So, too, their decisions may be colored by family loyalties, rivalries resentment etc. Resentments, jealousies, and outright hatred can emerge from the appointment. Hence the stage is set for later dispute, challenge, distrust, and a general dissipation of assets in the defense of it all.

For example, a beneficiary of a trust expressed great relief that her parents' trust terminated on the death of her parents. While her parents were alive, she was the designated co-trustee along with her sister, and so she was well aware of the problems that could happen. Her sister had been jealous of her for years and was using her mother's death as an opportunity to manipulate her regarding a division of her mother's jewelry and assets. She was horrified to think that, had the trust continued, her sister would have the ability to make decisions over money that was to go to her and her daughter. She could not imagine how people with complex trusts survived under the legal tyranny of family members in charge of family money.

In another family, the outcome was unfortunately not a "what if" but a hard reality. The grantor designated a trusted friend in charge of his assets by granting him complete discretion in his dealings with his family and the assets. The trustee chose to liquidate the family home on his friend's death over the objections of the beneficiaries and family who wanted to retain it. The trustee did not want to bother with the disputes that arose over management of real property and wanted to reduce his administrative tasks. The beneficiaries felt helpless to stop him and, for the most part, they were.

So too, family members are not the grantor. They may be a bit more equipped to play the parent role, but they do not always know how the grantor would handle certain issues or make decisions for his/ her trust. Decisions made may have no resemblance to the way the grantor would have decided the issues.

Finally, but certainly not the least problem with the personal fiduciary, is the fact that there is no independent oversight of his/her actions as trustee. Distributions may be sporadic, unpredictable, and undocumented. Goals of the grantor may be ignored. Many fail to provide the basic information required of a fiduciary. With litigation as the only control on the personal or professional trustee, there is no one to assure that the administration is being done correctly.

Because it is family in charge the beneficiaries become complacent and do not check on their representative for fear of family division or problems. When the beneficiaries find out about errors made by their trustee, the money or assets are often gone leaving the beneficiaries to try to recover the lost funds from an illiquid family trustee.

Paying your Trustee

Being a trustee is a hard job no matter if that person is a personal friend, relative, or a trust officer in an institution. And while I have been quick to point out that banks are charging far more in fees than they advertise, I must stress that because of all the work a trustee does, he/she/it should be paid.

However, paying the trustee is not actually part of the trust tradition. In earlier times when trusts were only something the very wealthy used, a trustee gladly took on the role of trustee because it meant prestige and social position as well as access to the wealthy. This prompted the wealthy to assume that one would work selflessly for little or no pay for raising another's children, dealing with their financial issues, and preserving their assets. The commercial banks that once served as trustee for well-to-do customers found, over time, that the time commitment for managing the assets and decisions regarding family money and assets was a thankless job. It placed them in a no-win position of family arbitrator, often cost them money, and exposed them to liability for little if any reward. As well, many of the trustees would attest to being abused by their charges. Children with little to no motivation to work because of family wealth made demands for funds to support their spoiled or decadent lifestyles. These children squandered family fortunes for which the trustee became responsible. Because of this, guidelines and conditions had to be established through expensive court proceedings and a trustee that declined to distribute funds often put the trustee in the cross hairs for attack by the unhappy beneficiaries. Constant demands for information, demands for funds, general solicitations of the trustee for favors from the trust, and unreasonable levels of expectation of performance and exposure of personal assets for mistakes made the trustee position unattractive to most. In short, the role of trustee has rarely been a desirable one.

Even where control over family money makes the person powerful and grants him or her a certain prestige as controller of the funds, reality is that this is a difficult job at best and, at worst, can cause personal loss as a result of litigation and surcharge for poor performance. Further, it is a time-consuming job that requires training and a level of business acumen not enjoyed by most.

One should not expect service for free. After all, how many of us want to sacrifice our own time, energy, and livelihood for the thankless position of making financial, family, and life decisions for another? Some would say there is not enough money in the world that could make them do this job. Others do it selflessly, but resentment often invades their thinking, particularly where the beneficiaries constantly second guess decisions made on their behalf.

Today, it should be recognized that the job of trustee is truly a job and not a favor. Do not expect your loved ones or friends to step into this thankless role without a structure that will compensate them for their time and the work performed. Unfortunately, few recognize how difficult and time consuming it is for a personal representative to administer a trust, and so they believe that the person they name will step forward to serve out of duty and loyalty. We also don't want to face up to the fact that the people we place in the position of trustee may have little incentive to administer our estate or trust at all. There is no real upside for the personal representative for the services he/she/it provides. The work is demanding, time

> **Technology Teaser**
>
> In fact, with emotionless technology designed to catch errors and minimize loss, trustworthiness is taken out of the equation.
>
> With electronic safeguards, the assets are not lost, investments are monitored, and frauds are caught. I often say when describing the emerging technology, that the fox can be in the hen house, but he will only get to eat one chicken before he is caught.

consuming, thankless, and carries with it personal liability for administrative mistakes.

Because the job of trustee is, ultimately, thankless, more and more the model of selfless trustee is disappearing in favor of the trustee for hire. Services rendered are to be paid for, and the required expertise is either developed at the expense of the trust or purchased as needed with trust funds. We should expect to pay for services rendered; however, we have to make sure the services we are paying for are rendered for the benefit of the trust and its beneficiaries.

Are Our Expectations Realistic?

A great failure of the current system is the assumption that whoever we place in charge of our estate or trust will do it well and selflessly, and will strive to accomplish our goals. We think our trustee will learn or obtain the requisite skills and training necessary to wind the estate through the administrative process successfully and inexpensively so that our assets are preserved and distributed to our named beneficiaries. As anyone with sense should tell you, these assumptions are simply unrealistic. The errors in decisions that are seemingly ignored or tolerated for a period of years have a cumulative effect. The buildup of perceived offenses in the administration may appear to be ignored or forgiven by the beneficiaries until a precipitating event ignites the resentment and anger. Then the trust or estate erupts into litigation and removal proceedings with everything from demands for restoration of the losses over the years to punitive damages for alleged-knowing fraud in the administration. When Mom or Dad was in charge, we recognized their shortcomings and allowed for them. But when it is our sister, brother, cousin, uncle, or some unnamed professional who has power over Mom or Dad's wealth, we are less forgiving.

If there is anything I have learned in this business of trusts and estates, it is that where money, assets, and control are concerned, all of humankind's most negative traits emerge. This is true on all sides of the equation. Just as the trustees express intolerance for grasping beneficiaries, those same beneficiaries have little patience or tolerance for their trustee's arbitrariness or incompetence. We have to recognize that by creating a trust, we have forced a relationship of trustee and beneficiary that none may appreciate or want. The trick to making it work is to make it predictable, transparent, and accountable. This neutralizes situations where a discretionary exercise of power is arbitrary, subjective, or abusive. That's the only way you can know that your trust and all those involved with it are truly trustworthy.

CHAPTER 6

The Professional Fiduciary–Banks:
The Problems they Create and
the Problems they Face

In the previous chapter, I touched on some of the problems you can run into with banks as your professional fiduciary. For instance, the professional fiduciary presents itself as a professional and is expected to perform as a professional. This means you may expect undivided loyalty, impartiality, accountability, transparency (they should hide nothing), and general honesty. However, what you and your beneficiaries typically get are printed accountings typical of financial institutions, a person to talk to on the phone, and some modicum of financial management by the money-management portion of the bank. You may or may not get a letter responding to your inquiries.

As I emphatically pointed out in chapter 5 as well, while we get the numbers, we don't get the decisions behind the numbers, and all too often the numbers raise more questions than they answer. Over the years, I've run into questions such as: Why was one asset sold and not another? Why was an investment made in Enron or PG&E? Did the trust manager sell these stocks upon seeing the warning signs that the companies were in trouble? Why was the family home sold at a loss when other assets were available for liquidation? Why were attorneys retained at the expense of the trust, and were they protecting beneficiaries or the financial interests of the bank? What work was done? Have bills been produced for the beneficiaries so they can see the work the trust is paying for? Why were charges incurred in the trust for insurance on real property that under the lease was required to be paid by the tenant? What work was performed for the 2 – 5 percent of assets under management? Why are the fees so high, and are there hidden unexplained fees in the administration?

While you are now aware that any trustee must provide by law some sort of accounting to the beneficiaries, many do not honor this requirement. But the problem is actually worse than that. When they do provide the accounting reports, oftentimes the reports are incoherent, so it is difficult to track the funds. All too often the accounting is done in bank language that is generally unintelligible to the beneficiaries. I've also seen some fishy tricks in the accounting documents because they don't have strict rules on the way reports should be done. Sometimes, banks make up categories in the accounting that do not track from year to year, and this makes it difficult to determine whether you are losing money in your trust or not. Sometimes, it is very hard to tell if all the assets are productive. If they are not, it's almost impossible to get an answer as to why. Banks may send a statement every month that shows that the assets may have gone up or down in value; however, they don't accompany the statement with a written report from the trust administrator explaining why the numbers are different and why the trust or estate has gained or lost money. They do not explain the decisions they have made, nor do they state if they have looked at your trust at all in the previous year. There is no analysis as to whether the grantor's goals are being reached and no stakes in the ground as to progress made or lost. In short, there is a vacuum of information. There is no standard articulated against which banks judge their own performance, and quite frankly, I am really tired of hearing the excuse that the market is to blame for their poor performance.

Part of the problem with the whole accounting system currently used by banks is the very fact that they don't have adequate accounting systems set in place. By reading this far into the book, you now have at least an idea of what you should expect from your relationship with a professional fiduciary. But to be fair and to help you understand the complexities of the issue I'm presenting, I want to give you a better idea of how the banks currently view your trust. But I also have to give you a warning: the last part of this chapter will get somewhat technical. It is really written for banks so that they, too, can be better informed of the real risks they face with the administration of our trusts. If you find yourself getting confused or feeling like you don't want to continue, by all means stop reading and move on to the next chapter. I don't want to lose you before I get to the chapters that offer you real solutions on how you can better handle your trust!

The Fiduciary Rules and Roles

The fiduciary obligation and rules of responsibility are relatively stringent, and of course we all want this kind of accountability when it is our money and family at stake. But how the rules play out tends to be very different from the ideal. I hope you know by now that if you think creating a trust creates a cocoon of safety where your children and families will be taken care of, you are in a dream world. It is only in that dream world that a trustee will analyze your beneficiary's individual needs and assure your assets are properly invested.

Since the fiduciary has not been provided specific implementation or execution plans, it rarely, if at all, prepares a plan for the trust that is individualized to the needs of the particular trust. If the fiduciary provides a plan, it is usually an investment plan that fits thousands of accounts under management. Professional fiduciaries simply do not have the manpower or any cost-effective method of meeting the individual needs of the accounts they service. Nor are they in the business of handholding like a parent would, responding to every demand of the people they serve.

Even for the $10 million-plus trust that commands the attention of the professional fiduciary, administration is rarely customized to the needs of the beneficiaries or trust. Instead, the attention given to this high-end client will normally be only as long as the grantor is around to monitor performance.

Looking at it from the bank's perspective, the benefits of being a trustee are relatively small. So when the goals of the trust or estate are unclear and directives ambiguous or vague, not surprisingly, the professional looks to the bottom line from its own perspective, e.g., whether your trust will be profitable for the bank. It all comes down to this hard reality: private client services—what the banks have named their trust departments—and wealth management equates to general investment management in the bank with some accounting functions.

Fees—A More In-Depth Look

As I stressed in the last chapter, it is important that your trustee get paid. However, what I strongly object to is when the professional fiduciary automatically withdraws fees from the trust's account, yet the work that was done on the trust does not warrant those fees. When I handled that initial trust case in San Francisco in 1984, the fees weren't automatically deducted from trusts. The banks had to present a bill, and the beneficiary could accept or object the fee based on the work that was done and the performance of the trustee. It kept everything a bit more on the up-and-up, but over the years the banks have gotten legislation passed that allows them to deduct fees before they have been approved by the beneficiaries. (This is the law that also allowed banks to invest in their own bank instruments.)

While you are already aware that the bank charges more fees than it initially advertises, it is important for you to understand all the different ways a bank assesses fees. Professional administrative fees range anywhere from 1.5 percent to 6.6 percent of the value of assets under management *annually*, but here's the catch. This does not mean the book value of assets, but the current fair-market value of assets under management. Hence that is why your assets are reappraised regularly. While it may appear at first glance that the initial fees for administration are between the advertised 1 – 2 percent, it is not long before you realize there are added fees for any number of services including, but not limited to, acceptance, correspondence, real property management, check writing, investment services, etc. In fact in one instance, bank administrative fees were doubled by charging the trust 2 percent of the value of the real property under management and then adding to this a 4 percent fee based on the gross-rental income of the same property. Oh, and fiduciary fees do not include attorney's fees, accountant's fees, tax preparation fees, appraisal fees, auction fees and charges, etc. But *all* of these fees will come out of your trust.

Let me give you an example of what I'm talking about. In one trust, the professional fiduciary provided financial statements regarding the assets under management and the basic ins and outs of the funds received. What it did not disclose in its accounting was the fact that it was paying no attention to the real property under management, simply collecting the rent, and paying itself a management fee. But the real hitch was when the bank acquired the property in the name of the trust; it failed to assess the fact that the commercial store site had a flooding problem. The flooding problem was well known to the seller of the property and the building department, but the professional fiduciary either failed to investigate this obvious problem before it purchased the property for the trust or simply ignored it. Unbeknownst to the beneficiaries of the trust, the property suffered yearly water damage, and the property was not worth the purchase price. When it was investigated, the problem turned out to be worse than expected because the entire drainage issue was a design issue as well. Because the trustee had agreed to assume all liability for design defects in the purchase contract and maintenance of the premises in the lease the trust was on the hook to pay for correction of the entire problem. The professional trustee that received its fees based on 2 percent of the fair-market value of the property formula plus 4 percent of the gross annual rent suffered none of the losses sustained by the trust. While the trust was required to pay for all of the correction work, the professional trustee suffered only in less income received during this process.

As it stands now, you need to look at the simple but tough question: Will your trust be able to withstand the fees associated with professional administration? You need to figure out to what extent the annual fiduciary fee burn depletes your trust principal and compromises the goals you have set. In addition, you should count on additional fees for advisors, lawyers, accountants, and tax preparations.

Oh, and by the way, here's a tip: when you request that your professional trustee send a written report explaining its accounting and investments, it will probably not be prepared to respond to such a request because professional trustees do not count on this kind of accountability. They may even threaten to charge extra fees for the work. Nonetheless, insist this information be provided at no extra charge because in reality it is the bank's duty to give you this information. And know that if we all start insisting on this level of accountability, the standard in the industry will begin to move more into compliance with the law.

The IRS Breakdown

When I discovered that the fees banks charge are far higher than what they advertise, I got alarmed and went sleuthing. I went to the IRS website, http://www.irs.gov/pub/irs-soi/05fallbu.pdf, to look up "fiduciary income tax returns" for filing years 2003-2004. (The IRS lags four years behind the current year.) I knew that the IRS requires professional fiduciaries to file fiduciary returns on behalf of the trusts and estates they administer. They must disclose in these returns the fiduciary fees received as they serve as deductions to the trust or estate they administer, and so I knew I would get a truer picture of the actual charges against your trust or estate. Here is what I found: in 2003, nearly 3.7 million fiduciary income-tax returns were filed for income earned in 2002. In that year, trusts and estates reported gross income of $71.3 billion—that's a lot of money, folks! Now just like any other taxable income, estates and trusts may deduct expenses and fees paid to fiduciaries as well as those paid to attorneys, accountants, and return preparers for the purpose of determining taxable income to the trust or estate. Here's a breakdown of the deductions based upon the above findings: fiduciary fees accounted for 6.6 percent of the deductions, and attorney, accountant, and return-preparer fees accounted for an additional 5.1 percent of $59.0 billion in deductions taken. In short, 11.7 percent is annually taken out of the trust or estate in fees including attorney fees, accountant fees, and tax-return-preparer fees. Banks advertise they charge 1.5 percent in fees; however, in reality, they charge significantly more, and then they charge an *additional* amount for other professionals which is taken annually from your trust. Now these stats are not clean stats (because they include fiduciary fees for estates and bankruptcy estates), but they indicate that the fees are far greater than the 1.5 percent of assets under management frequently advertised.

Handling Assets

Part of what all these fees are supposed to cover is the professional fiduciary handling—meaning investing and managing—your assets. But what does that look like from the bank's perspective? One of the areas trust administrators often complain about is where the grantor has placed certain restrictions on the disposition or sale of certain assets. In this regard there may be too many restrictions such that the management of assets is placed at risk. This is called a "concentration of assets." This occurs in situations where the grantor has restricted the sale of an asset, a home, the family farm, the family company, PG&E stock, etc. He or she instructs the trustee or administrator to retain the asset, anticipating that the asset will increase in value or will produce income similar to its current income generating capability. What has not been anticipated by the grantor are the future events that may compromise the value of the asset or the desire of the beneficiaries or trustee to liquidate. While the asset increases in value, all is well, but when the asset begins to lose market value or spiral into free-fall, the trustee is helpless to change the position of the trust or estate without violation of the grantor's directive. The trustee is placed in a Catch-22 position and is at risk in the administration of the trust or estate for the losses suffered.

Let me give you an example: In one instance, the grantor created a company that went public. He put in his trust a large chunk of the company stock that he instructed should be retained for the benefit of his children and grandchildren. About fifteen years later, the company's management changed because the grantor had died. The stock started to spiral downhill. The trustee was prohibited by the terms of the trust from selling the stock, so he petitioned the court to do so. The trustee was met with some objection from the beneficiaries who were convinced there would be a turn around and the trustee lost. The stock ultimately tanked, and the beneficiaries who wanted the stock sold turned on the trustee claiming that he should have gone back to court. How do you think the trustee felt after that attack?

In most cases, the grantor is not present to fix the problems he or she created. Do your trustee a favor. As the grantor, anticipate situations that could arise in relation to your assets, and set parameters for the sale and liquidation of any of your properties, no matter how loathe you are to let them go. It's more important to have a plan in place to deal with these circumstances. If it is too late to change your own trust documents, the trustee should modify the language through court proceedings to clarify the events that would allow liquidation and/or sale of assets should the need arise.

Standardization of Terms

In chapter 4, I griped about estate planners using form books to help them write trusts. The language in these books is often muddled at best and downright incomprehensible at worst. However, while I don't like form books, I do like the idea of standardizing the language used in trusts. Should the person leaving his or her assets in trust be called a "grantor" or a "settlor," for example? This will help all parties involved in the trust because when estate planners use different sets of terms, forms, definitions, and customization for their clients, the actual plans differ widely. So too we should have standard definitions for "health, education, and welfare" not to mention, support, maintenance and the myriad of other terms that are left to the trustee to define.

There is another problem that sits on the other side of this coin that can greatly affect who is willing and able to act as your trustee. If you make the language in your trust too obscure, if you customize it too much, the more *unlikely* it is that your will or trust will be implemented in the way you want. Some people get the idea they want their will or trust to be totally unique to them, to their needs, desires, and assets. With the advent of technology that I'm calling for (and which you are going to find out more about in the last chapter), there will be enough individuality in your trust or estate without using language that confuses your directives and muddies your administrative plan.

Also, the more obscure and personalized you make the administration of your trust, the more labor-intensive your trust becomes. For example, one trust provided that upon the death of one spouse, their joint-living trust would become irrevocable and could not be amended, altered, or revoked by any person. Later on in the same trust, there were terms granting to the surviving spouse the right to amend, revoke, or alter the trust in whole or in part. This language set the trust up for later problems and litigation.

In another trust the provisions provided for distributions to the beneficiaries for the general welfare of the child beneficiary. General welfare was never defined, so the trustee was left to guess what the general welfare of the child was. The now-grown beneficiary wanted trust funds to start a business. She already had her food, housing, and healthcare needs met. So did starting a business come under the term general welfare? Who is the arbiter of this provision, and how was the trustee to decide? The request was ultimately declined, but I've always wondered if it was the correct decision. General welfare could conceivably include gainful employment and fulfilling one's dreams by engaging in an entrepreneurial effort.

In fact, if you think you can make your professional trustee pay attention to your trust by making it really different from other trusts, you may be asking too much of your trustee. Whomever you place in charge may want to please you but may grow weary from provisions they deem impossible to accomplish. Also, the fees charged to your trust will *not* be reasonable by definition if *you* require too much of the administrator's time trying to accomplish unreasonable goals and wishes.

From the professional fiduciary's perspective, their attempts to standardize terms and applications often run afoul of the language contained in the trust instruments they are charged with administering. While I have derided the lack of individual attention professional fiduciaries pay individual trusts, I also know that it is acceptable for professional fiduciaries to apply some form of standardization to their administration so their job of administration is not unwieldy for the thousands of trusts they hold. You should anticipate this type of standardization as it is unrealistic to expect a trust officer who handles anywhere from fifty to one hundred and fifty or more trusts to customize his administration all around your wants, needs, and desires.

For most of us, we have no idea whether the person we designate will actually do the job for which they have been assigned. Yet this same person or entity wields enormous power over the assets of our estates and the financial future of the beneficiaries and heirs they are to serve.

Providing guidance in the fiduciary's decision making may save them from lawsuits in the handling of your trust and save your beneficiaries loss of assets.

Risk to the Trustee of Administration

I don't think I need to reiterate the risk a grantor takes with his or her trust when appointing a trustee, especially if the grantor has not clearly designed a plan and its implementation. In chapter 5, I also outlined the real risk banks take on when they consent to handle a trust. It has to do with operational risk (the risk associated with day-to-day operations, the people, and the systems running a bank), but I'm going to delve deeper into the problems a trustee assumes that are associated with that risk.

There are, in fact, many levels of risk a trustee takes on when administering a trust. With each decision a trustee makes without clear direction from the grantor, the trustee is exposed to potential liability. It is a liability that may play out over time because the beneficiaries may not notice any inconsistencies right away, but it is liability and risk nonetheless.

Trustee's View of Risk

Professional fiduciaries are aware of the operational risks they take on. But with so many trusts assigned to each trust officer, many view their job as impossible with emphasis placed on generating customers rather than servicing the clients. There is recognition that literally hundreds of trusts are not looked at but are still charged the 1.5 – 2 percent administrative fee.

Trust officers also have few tools with which to do their job. Technology is at best backwater. While the accounting function is relatively sophisticated, the actual administrative tools are few and archaic. File drawers bulge with paper, and three-ring-binder mentalities dominate. The only computing power comes in the form of Excel spreadsheets, and in-house, hands-on review of a trust's documents. This is a recipe for disaster and is compounded by the fact that training of the personal fiduciary is recognized as substandard. In one interview, the trust officer complained the bank was simply taking people off the street who knew nothing about trusts but who were good salesmen to get trust customers in the door. Even the training groups that offer services to the professional fiduciary confess that they only give an overview of trust administration and admit to the inadequacy of such training.

Lack of internal expertise for the management of trust assets causes additional problems. While the assets may provide a large number on the books of the financial institution for its assets under management, and the fees may be attractive, the lack of requisite skills in the management of the asset sets the stage for later loss and subsequent lawsuits.

Significant inefficiencies with no standardized way of dealing with any of it places the fiduciary at risk for second guessing and subsequent attack. From a higher view of the trust department, board members as well as presidents of financial institutions regard the trust department as a black box. They cannot get a handle on this black box because each trust, its beneficiaries, assets, directives, and expectations are unique to the grantor who created it. There is no one-size-fits-all administrative program that can deal uniformly with any trust—let alone thousands of them. So the trustees get by with what they have. As long as no one is doing a better job, the standard stays the same. But substandard fiduciary services that fail to meet customer expectations simply alienate the very people and businesses the fiduciary wants to attract. Nor is it any longer a secret that people are becoming wise to these inadequacies.

Risk reduction has come a long way for the financial institutions with the application of Basel 2 risk reduction criteria (risk reduction recommendations for the banking operation as a whole as based on the Basel Committee on Banking's recommendations), but the area of trust administration still suffers from unidentified risk. Since there is no real grasp of the risk involved in trust administration, which is generally higher than currently accounted for, many financial institutions are looking at fewer but more profitable high-end trusts as a means of reducing their exposure. Many are vying for the $5 million and above trust for two reasons. The $1 million trust requires all the administrative skills and acumen brought to the $5 million trust, but the $5 million trust can afford to pay for the service, and the $1 million trust cannot. Second, the smaller trust assets may be consolidated with other smaller trusts into an investment plan or package that fits the bank's service model rather than accommodate the individual administration expected by the grantor. However, this exposes the trustee to the risk of not addressing the individual goals, needs, and plans associated with the smaller trust—and it is a risk the trustee and beneficiary alike should be aware of.

> *Warning: What follows is specifically written for banks. It outlines the risk banks need to be aware of when they take on the job of trustee.[3]*

Traditional Risk

The organization and structure of a financial institution typically divides itself into five divisions: corporate, retail, asset management, insurance, and support. Because trusts historically have been the stepchild of most financial institutions, there is no division specific to trust administration. Instead, services provided have become a hybrid of other divisions of the bank.

Corporate banking encompasses service to large corporate clients in the form of underwriting, trades and sales, mergers and acquisitions, commercial lending, and research. The retail division services the personal bank customers taking deposits, servicing checking, savings, and fixed deposit accounts, and lending funds to customers in the form of mortgages, credit accounts, and personal loans. Private banking may fall into both the corporate division and retail banking as it provides special services in the form of loans, investment management, and trading services to the high-end customer. The asset-management group administers funds in the form of unit trusts, mutual funds, etc. The asset-management group manages money that does not belong to the bank, and this is often where trust administration currently falls. The insurance division takes a fee from its customers for specific insurance against the occurrence of a specific event. This can be in the form of property, casualty, life, and/or commercial insurance. Trust administration does not fit easily into any one of these categories but overlaps them all.

---

3   This section was co-written with Ernest Freeman

Risk Covered by the OCC

The Office of the Comptroller of the Currency (OCC) has issued a *Handbook for Personal Fiduciary Services* that affirmatively states, "Personal fiduciary services create risk to a bank that must be identified, measured, controlled and monitored." It describes the risk as "potentially unlimited" because "each account is a separate legal relationship that involves unique client characteristics and fiduciary duties and responsibilities"(OCC Handbook 30-31).

Risk factors that apply to personal fiduciary services from the perspective of the OCC include: transaction, compliance, reputation, and strategic risk.

- **Transaction Risk:** Transaction risk addresses the processing and reporting of transactions. The OCC measures success on how well the fiduciary gathers, reports, and processes transactions and information. Transaction risk includes: transactions, information, and accounting reports in the form of accepting and establishing accounts; receipt and disbursement of income; purchase, sale, valuation, and investment performance measurement; review and execution of discretionary distribution; maintenance of account records, preparation and distribution of client statements; preparation and submission of account tax returns and reports; preparation of internal financial records and reports. Transaction risk involves the nuts and bolts of trust administration at the execution stage.

- **Compliance Risk:** Compliance risk encompasses conducting administration within federal, state, and local laws and complying with the trust instrument, agency agreements, wills, court orders, etc. Compliance with law encompasses not only trust and probate law but also securities, tax, environmental, consumer protection, criminal law, etc. Compliance also includes regulatory agencies, bank policies, operating procedures, and control systems. Again this is at the execution stage of the trust.

- **Strategic Risk:** This risk applies to the business-plan side of banking and encompasses sound strategic planning embraced by the board of directors and senior management. It includes decisions whether to make acquisitions, develop products and services in-house, or to retain other firms. It deals with development of information systems, hiring staff or experts, product development, designating distribution channels, and development of internal control systems. By the way, here is where they decide to invest in technology to apply to their trust departments. This area relates to the bank and how it is run. It impacts your trust only tangentially as it is here where decisions are made whether to adopt emerging technology that could facilitate the administration of your trust.

- **Reputation Risk:** Success in providing personal fiduciary services depends in part on the reputation enjoyed by the fiduciary. A good reputation is essential in attracting and retaining fiduciary accounts. According to the OCC, risk to reputation is dependant upon the bank's ability to manage transaction, compliance, and strategic risk. Below-average investment performance, poor service quality, poor planning, or weak initiatives are viewed as leading to diminished reputation and an inability to compete.

Banks Lose Money by Taking on Too Much Risk

Risk in traditional banking terms, what I defined in the previous chapter as market risk, credit risk, and operating risk, is a little different than the OCC's definitions of risk, and it is instructive to revisit them here. If you ask anyone from a bank's trust department to categorize the risk inherent in their trust administration, he or she will tell you that the risk faced does not fall into any one or any three of the traditional risk categories. The closest category utilized is operational risk, but this category fails to do justice to the risks inherent in this sector of the bank.

Trusts are hit with many types of risk including Sarbanes Oxley, the Patriot Act, and privacy and security regulations, among others such as risk of failure in trust administration and therefore loss to the bank. Risk also comes from the trust instruments themselves, mainly in their language. The broad discretionary authority coveted by many actually places the trustee's judgment between the cross hairs for liability and sets the trustee up for loss. Inconsistent terms, ambiguities, authorized favoritism, unequal treatment of beneficiaries, and broad directives, to name a few, provide the foundation for later problems. Additional risk for loss can be attributed to the history of the trust which encompasses the actions of the grantor or former trustees. A waiver of liability for actions of the predecessor does not adequately protect the successor trustee from the ripple effect of bad decisions, erroneous interpretations, and financial losses that carry into the successor's administration. So, too, the beneficiaries themselves add risk to the equation with their history, background, goals, disputes, family rivalries, etc. When you add normal operating risk to this formula, you begin to understand the complexity of trust administration. The travesty of it all is that at least 50 – 60 percent of the risk is not covered by normal banking risk analysis or risk assessment and cannot easily be identified by the auditors.

Because Basel 2 risk categories do not address the above risks, it is not hard to see why trust administration carries significant risk of loss and unpredictability in administration. Efforts at standardization in the trust arena have often met with disastrous consequences. For example, when one major financial institution tried to streamline the fee structure of its acquired bank, it was not too long before an industrious attorney asserted that the trust instruments were not amenable to such conformity and a class-action suit resulted in a $150 million-plus price tag. Banks have retreated from the standardized approach by promising personal service and customized administration. But with an average of fifty to one hundred and fifty trusts per trust officer, the promise of personal hand holding has given way to screening for trusts that can pay for personal attention even when it is not provided. Although banks today vie for the high-end trust, the available big trusts simply cannot support the number of financial institutions competing for their business.

The smarter bet is on the average $1.1 million trust, but this includes finding a way to service it economically and efficiently, so it is done right. Here is the challenge and here is where the introduction of technology can provide answers that have stumped the financial services industry for decades.

It is the business of the bank and its board of directors to oversee and manage the risk inherent in all sections of the bank. In this regard, the board is often urged to take risk by its shareholders who are seeking high returns. Yet the board is constrained by rating agencies, regulators, debt holders, legal requirements, and their own desire to assure that the bank stays in business. Balancing the risks and maximizing return on the risk is the balancing act of every financial institution.

In the last chapter of this book, I will outline how desktop software systems can support administrative tasks in a way that reduces the risks banks take on that are associated with trusts and provide the clients they serve with greater accountability, and services our fiduciaries should be providing today.

PART THREE

Take Matters Into Your Own Hands: It's Up to Us to Solve Our Trust Problems

Are you incensed yet? When I first started finding out about all the problems associated with trusts, I had a hard time believing the whole system that revolved around trusts could be so out of whack. But it is, and the problems seem to be getting worse. Just the other day, I had a couple in my office who were just lost. They had paid $3,500 to have their trust done, but when they got it back, it was a mess. The terms were inconsistent, the names of their children were wrong as well as their addresses. The directives they had wanted weren't in the document and even their assets had not been listed correctly or directed as instructed.

I have talked to many in the system, the representatives of the OCC (Office of the Comptroller of the Currency), bank officers and presidents, bank auditors, beneficiaries, estate planners, lawyers, and even technologists in the industry. Most acknowledge the problems they see, and most even applaud that something is finally being done about them. But each is concerned about their own segment of the industry and they are unwilling to fund change. When you think about it, why should they be interested in fixing the system? The government has set up some pretty decent laws surrounding trusts, and I'm sure these various entities believe that it's up to the beneficiaries to make sure the laws are enforced. But they know as well as I do that the beneficiaries usually neither have the wherewithal or the knowledge to adequately police this industry.

I am always amazed that while banks know about the problems inherent in the current trust system, they're not interested in changing it. They make too much money with the system set up as it is. One trust officer even had the audacity to say to me, "We are not feeling any pain." In other words, they don't want to change it. The estate lawyers and planners, while they are interested in having their plans work, also make money in the current system and have little incentive to make it change. In short, it is you and I who will feel the loss; it is our money and our family that are at stake, so it is up to us to change the system.

So what is the solution? Short of using the emerging trust technology that I have been working to develop (see fiduciarytechnologiesinc.com) when you form your estate plan, you should be able to articulate what you want it to accomplish and have in place an implementation plan. Remember, the problems in a trust can only be seen in the execution stage, but the solutions lie in the way the plan is specified, its design attached to an implementation plan. As I have said throughout this book, the solutions to many of the problems associated with trusts are contained within the trust document itself and how you set it up. You need to establish enough information about beneficiaries and assets to set boundaries within which the trustee is to operate. Only with clearly defined goals and values, with specific language on what can and cannot be done, will the laws surrounding trusts be consistently enforceable.

What I'm about to share with you in part three is radical stuff—at least from the system's point of view. I'm going to give you solutions that will help you take more control of your estate. I'm going to take you step-by-step through how to set up your trust correctly so you have something concrete to take to your estate lawyer. I'm also going to offer what I think is the single best solution to this whole mess—creating a computerized system whereby each individual is able to set up a trust based on his or her own personal wants and needs but doing it in such a way that is easy, affordable, and workable for all parties involved.

As you read these solutions and think about how you want to implement them into your own estate plan, know something—it might be a rough road. You're going to find that the estate planners are going to look at you cross-eyed and complain loudly. They may even tell you that what you're asking for can't be done. Don't listen to any of their protests. Either make them comply with your wishes, or find another estate planner who is willing to set up a trust that will work for you. On the administration side, especially if you have named a bank as your trustee, you might find that no one will administer your trust. They just want you to sign your rights away via waivers and start collecting their fees. Just keep looking for an administrator who will do what you ask.

It really comes down to this: if the system is going to change, it has to change with us—a true grassroots kind of movement. So as you read this last segment of the book, know that to ultimately change the system either a bank or someone who is willing and able to form a trust company needs to come forward and say, "We'll do it differently." Because this is what's going to happen (in my professional opinion): once one company or bank does it the right way and everyone sees how it works, the industry will have to change. Otherwise we have to change it one step at a time through the way we plan and implement our trusts.

When the system has reformed, there will be plenty of estate planners who are willing to incorporate your design and implementation plans into your trust. With an execution/administrative plan for the trustee to follow, the personal or the professional trustee will know how to proceed, thus preventing many of the liabilities they face and we will be able to rest easy that we have a workable plan in place. Since almost all of the decisions would already be predetermined by the grantor, all the frustrations of administration will be relieved. If the beneficiary doesn't like the way the benefit is being distributed or invested, the trustee can simply and legally say: "I'm not the decision maker; your dad made the decision to lock your benefits. I'm just the caretaker."

Also, with a clear execution plan that is digitized, the beneficiaries are happier and more compliant because they have access to it. Their benefits are predictable. They'll know what hoops they have to jump through to get them. They'll be able to track the decisions and performance of their trustee. When the trust establishment adopts this technology, the investment side of a trust will be better handled as well. The system will be transparent. No more back-room committee decisions that thwart your beneficiaries' access to the benefits you left them, and you will know what benefits you can afford to leave. Performance of the investment will be monitored, and they can be made more flexible. Investment outcome can be predicted and monitored by the beneficiaries and trustee to see whether goals are being met.

The solutions I'm going to offer you ultimately put much of the responsibility for your trust on you, where it should be. If you aren't willing to take that responsibility, you are certainly welcome to use the system as it is currently set up and suffer the consequences. However, for the brave souls among you, follow what I outline in the following chapters, and you and your family may be better off for it. It really isn't that difficult. In essence, what you're doing is making it easy for your trustee to do his/ her job. Your estate or trust will be administered better if you tell your administrator what you want and expect and how you would decide issues regarding your trust. In the ideal world, you will have anticipated and addressed the events requiring decisions saving your fiduciary from erroneous calls, petitions to the court, or decisions that do not follow what you would do. In short, with good planning, the money you have set aside in your trust can benefit your beneficiaries, just as you wanted it to.

CHAPTER 7
Setting Up Your Trust

Setting up an estate plan, in the end, isn't rocket science. It is something that requires a lot of planning and a great attention to detail. While my ultimate solution involves the use of computer technology that is not yet available (because I need funding to make it happen), there are many positive things you can do right now to set up an estate plan that works. The following is the step-by-step process I would like to see happen with every trust that is created. It is designed to allow you to plan for the worst because while the assumption is that everyone is competent, does the right thing, is fiscally responsible, and can be trusted, the reality is different. I always say, plan for the worst and hope for the best. Assume that your assets will be taken, that people aren't to be trusted, and this will make you plan differently.

Step One: Inventory Everything

Assets: In order to plan for your assets under all contingencies (e.g., their sale, disputes involving them, lost assets, asset liquidation to meet taxes, unequal division of assets, assets held for future need, etc.), it is vital that you keep a current inventory of all your assets—in other words, your stuff. This includes all your material goods as well as any ownership documents that prove you are the owner.

When you inventory your assets, this includes writing them down, taking pictures, and valuing it all. You must also have some proof of each asset's value. Either you show a receipt for each item, or you have it appraised. I consider anything over $5,000 in value to be a big ticket item requiring appraisal.

A current appraisal is important because it sets a value for your administrator to start with. If the appraisal is within three years of your death, it can be used to contest a higher IRS valuation. Advise your appraiser that you want a "fair market" valuation. While the appraiser is able to perform an "estate-value" appraisal that gives a low value for your items. This can backfire especially if it's a big-ticket item. The IRS is wise to these tricks, and they will come in and dispute the appraisal if it appears too low. You also want to be sure that your appraiser will testify truthfully that he took the fair-market value.

The reason you want to take pictures of everything you have put into your estate is so your administrator can match the picture with each item. Remember, I'm preparing you for the worst, and the truth is when you get old, people come in and take your stuff. You also want to be careful about what goes into a trust because it will all be accounted for by the government. You want to put real property, stocks and bonds, and those sorts of things into the trust. I think the best thing to do with the rest of your stuff is to give it away before you die, so your estate does not have to pay estate tax on it. Keep only the minimum that you value and treasure because, at your death, everything will go into your estate, and your estate will pay taxes on it.

I have seen it happen over and over; when a person dies, their books, antiques, jewelry, and even their furniture are sold off so that money can be put in the trust. Remember, under the current estate-tax laws, you can give up to $12,000 worth of tax-free gifts annually to each of your children or to anyone else you choose. So say you have a vintage Ford truck. It's now an heirloom because it was your father's truck, and you want to give it to your son. Give it to your son now, but first have it appraised. If its value is under $12,000, there will be no tax to pay. If it is over, you will pay gift tax only on the amount that is over. After you know the value, sign the title over to him—but this doesn't mean that you can't use the truck. Simply make an agreement with him that you will still be able to use it. Your son will have to pay for the licensing, but that guarantees he will get the heirloom instead of it being sold to pay estate taxes. The same goes for any jewelry, antiques, art, etc.

Now when you get into high-dollar gifts, the government will slap the gift tax onto anything over $12,000. Say you have an eight-carat diamond ring worth $50,000. You give it to your daughter before you die. She'll have to pay taxes on the remaining $38,000, but that's better than paying taxes on $50,000, isn't it? And, again, you'll ensure that she gets the asset you want her to have.

Some argue that you should keep your assets because in 2009 and 2010, for example, you can give away up to $2 million dollars to your kids on your death and not have it be taxed. In 2010 there is no estate tax. So assets given away in that year by your estate does so without tax consequence, *but* the capital gains tax is not repealed so when your heir sells that asset he/she will have to pay capital gains tax on that item. The numbers change depending on the year of your death (see the tax table in chapter 2). What it comes down to is that while you don't ultimately know what you're going to need to keep you comfortable in your later years, it's best to either give your assets away or sell them, and then pare down what remains. As you get older, give as much as you can to your family while you are alive so your children can reap the full benefits.

Debts: Part of your inventory must include what you owe. If you have a mortgage, credit-card debt, personal debt, contractual obligations, etc. at your death your estate will be responsible for it. Plan how to pay it from your estate. I once had a woman in my office who had no idea her husband was fiscally irresponsible. He had huge debts about which she was unaware. She had to pay the debt because she was legally responsible for it as it was incurred during their marriage. If you are married, make sure you have a handle on marriage debts. It does not serve you well to be blindsided by your partner's irresponsibility.

Ownership Documents: Saying that you need to account for everything you own in your inventory might sound silly. Of course you own your house or your car. However, ownership issues are not always so clear cut. Say you have a house you own in common with your live-in partner, married or not. When you die, unless you have designated your share of the house to go to your partner, he or she will only have a percentage interest in the house and your estate will have the other. The IRS will swoop in, value your share, assess your estate for the taxes, and your estate may have to sell the house to be able to pay the taxes. To avoid that fate, check ownership documents and talk to your lawyer. He may advise putting the house in joint tenancy if you want it to go to your partner. Also check on ownership issues that may cloud the title to your property. Resolve these issues before you die. Further, if you live in a community-property state, you will want to know whether the asset in question is separate or community proper (property acquired during marriage is presumed community property). If it was acquired prior to marriage, it must be kept separate and not commingled (combined with other community property) to keep its separate property status.

Find out what you own outright. Do you share an interest in property, a business, or both? Are you a shareholder? Are you a limited partner? Ownership issues encompass both property and businesses, and there's a whole slew of different kinds of ownership designations. For example, there is the "life" designation where you have the use of a property for life; "fee simple" where you own something outright; or "contingent interest" where your ownership of something is contingent on another event happening or not. The terms get very confusing, so I'm not going to give any more of them to you here. Just know that if you have an ownership interest in a business or property, check with the entity or with your other partners. Ask them for copies of the documents that created the entity, and make sure everything is clear in those documents about what happens to your interest when you die.

For instance, if you have invested in a medical partnership or practice, how much of that practice do you own, and what will happen to that when you die? Look at the documents you signed, and see what provisions are in them for your estate. If there are no provisions, get the partnership to write specific provisions into the document dealing with what happens if a partner dies. If you don't, your estate could be tied up in long and even nasty litigation trying to extricate your interests (or shares) from the other surviving partners or business owners.

Contractual Agreements: Next, you need to examine any kind of personal agreements you have with others that could impact your ownership, things like a prenuptial agreement or any postnuptial agreement with your spouse or live-in partner. For example, a gay couple or a couple in a common-law marriage should have a contract with each other regarding the ownership of jointly held property. I actually urge all non-married couples to have these kinds of contracts because out-of-marriage relationships do not share the same rights as married couples.

Get Your trust in e-Format: When your estate planner gives you your trust, insist that you get a copy in electronic form. The electronic copy will allow you to take advantage of emerging technology that will analyze your trust, screen it for risk, and link it to an administrative plan.

Step Two: Figuring Out Estate Taxes

Once you know what your assets are and who owns what, you need to talk to an accountant or tax attorney and get a feel for what your estate taxes are going to be if you die tomorrow. This info will tell you two things: how much of your estate you will need to liquefy to pay taxes and how much of your estate will be left to give away. Many times people have called me because the family farm or the beloved family home was up for sale because the estate taxes had to be paid. There's nothing I can do in that instance. You *must* provide a way to pay the estate taxes, and that means you should designate which assets are going to be sold to meet this liability. By analyzing this step early, it also gives you a chance to do damage control and minimize losses by giving away assets, restructuring ownership, etc.

I also know that the sad truth is there are some people who don't care what happens when they die. They think, "I've lived my life, enjoyed it, and I don't care what happens with my money and my stuff." If you think this way, please at least consider what I'm about to say. If you don't plan for at least some of the obvious issues that arise, like estate taxes and high-dollar assets, someone will have to do your dirty work of deciding what gets sold and who gets the remainder. And if you take this route, you will create generations who hate you. I know of one lawyer who tried to get his uncle to restructure his estate so all was not lost to the government. The uncle refused and left a huge mess at his death. This was years ago, but the animosity and disdain is still there and will be for a long time. To leave it up to your heirs to handle your estate issues is selfish. And, really, how is it right to leave to others what you should be handling yourself?

Step Three: Setting Up a Living Will

I have talked briefly about the living will (again this is different from a living trust) in chapter 1 and the problem of not having one in chapter 4. This is one aspect of estate planning that no one should overlook. A living will allows you to speak when you've been incapacitated and can't speak for yourself. If you don't have a living will in place, the court will search for someone who can speak for you. Usually, your spouse or your parents are automatically given the right to speak for you, but what happens if they can't be found right away? Emergency care can remain in limbo until directives can be given. These are medical directives for the car accident, the coma, the mishap that snatches us from consciousness. Everyone who has minor children, for example, should have a living will, no matter how old the children are, so that in case you are in an accident and can't care for them, their care is specifically laid out.

For example, when my daughter was really young, I had to go to the hospital because I was in a hyper-allergic state. This meant I had to get transfusions so that my immune system would be strengthened. I had my daughter with me in the hospital in the waiting room. When I was called in for treatment, she wanted to stay and finish watching her TV program, so I asked a nurse to watch her. Once the program was over, my child started getting anxious, but the nurses didn't allow her in to see me. She started becoming hysterical, and when I heard her, I insisted she be allowed in with me. My husband was out of town, so he wasn't able to be there with her. It was a potentially ugly situation, but I was lucky that I still was able to talk. However, if I had not been able to speak, and I had not specifically left instructions as to what I wanted for my daughter she would have been left with a social worker or other. And it could have been worse. Say I was in a coma? Who would take care of my daughter? Who would pick her up from the hospital, or day-care, or from school? Where would she stay at night?

You want a well-orchestrated plan in place for you and for your children in case of emergency. Put it all in your living will, even who will be responsible for paying your mortgage. (The mortgage holders don't really care if you're on your deathbed; they want their money.) Technology will help here. All this information can be accessible on line. Absent technology it should be readily accessible in the case of emergency. I've created a living will template that contains areas to address all of these issues. You are welcome to download it at www.SueFarley.com. By all means, check it with your attorney so it meets your needs.

Step Four: Setting-up Your Own Care in a Living Trust

As I have said before, make sure you have provided for your own care. As you start thinking about how you want your assets distributed, do not make the mistake of assuming your will or trust will only go into effect when you die. Your trust may go into effect when you are no longer able to care for your own day-to-day living. Giving everything away and thinking others will take care of you is frequently a mistake. Today, few take care of their aging parents and leave this job to the rest homes or care facilities. Make sure you have enough for your own health care, maintenance, in-home assistance, meal preparation, entertainment, etc. Anticipate that you will require this assistance. The simple truth about aging is that we do not always recognize that we are failing. Remember your spouse will be aging with you, so a dual plan of support should be discussed. Finally, if you don't want your heirs simply putting you in a rest home and taking what you have, make sure to set up a plan that works for you, not for them.

The best vehicle through which your own care is set up is the living (revocable) trust, but it can also be done through a complex trust or through health directives and financial directives in your living will. The living trust ensures you're taken care of when you become infirm. You spell out as many parameters and directives for your own care that you can address. If you want to stay at home, you need to specify who will care for you, who will find a care provider, who will write checks for you, pay your bills, advocate for you, and monitor your care.

I know from personal experience of taking care of my infirm grandmother that you need to stay on top of in-home-care providers.

Say you have a mother with Alzheimer's. You hire an agency to send you a care giver, the agency sends someone but this person proceeds to watch TV all day while your mother lies in bed doing nothing. For $20 to $35per hour the caregiver needs to be doing laundry, fixing meals, cleaning the bathrooms and kitchen, taking your mother to the beauty parlor, to friends, to the s senior centers, lectures, or physical therapy sessions. In short, you want to make sure that these care providers are giving your infirm parent a daily routine that is stimulating. Make provisions for your own entertainment. Many old people do not have the capability of entertaining themselves or setting up activities, and thus they have nothing to do. Designate what activities you want to participate in: golf, swim, play mahjong, senior programs etc. Specifically state you want to be transported to the senior center twice a week, visit friends, visit family etc. Also specify how your estate will pay for all of this. (Some opt to purchase long-term care that will take care of some of these types of expenses.)

From experience, both with my own grandmother and handling cases that involve infirm elderly people, I know that other people are generally not interested in helping you when you're old and infirm with even some of the basics such as your food or medical needs. They certainly don't want to be handling your temper tantrums or abuse, a common occurrence with aging people. There are precious few who have a commitment to you, and to know what I mean, just visit an assisted-living facility or a nursing home. It is populated with people who get visits from family once a month or once a year because the family is too busy or thinks the parent doesn't love them anymore. This is especially true with an abusive or cranky parent. You'll happily take care of a cranky child because they get better. But when it's a parent, it's different because he or she doesn't get better. And a word of caution: if you have parents who are aging, don't ever think they don't know who you are or don't love you because they get mean. Never talk yourself into believing that they don't appreciate your care or attention. Like a child knows mother's voice, your parents know your voice. Whether or not they respond is dependent upon how sick they are, but please don't ever abandon your parent in their time of need. And also, think very hard about declaring your sick parent incompetent. Once a person is declared incompetent, they can't vote; they can't speak for themselves; they cannot make decisions for themselves; and they can't even talk to their doctor for themselves. All of their rights are taken away. They are completely subject to those who have been given power over them. In this regard they become vulnerable, and people see this as an opportunity to take advantage of them. It also robs the person's dignity. So in your living trust or letters of instruction, name someone who will be constantly vigilant and who is willing to care for you when you cannot.

Step Five: Talk to Your Children

At this point, you have a good idea of what you have and are thinking about how you want to divide your assets. However, before you actually sit down and start drafting your estate plan, talk to your children first. Communicate with them your thoughts on how you're structuring your estate so that you can avoid family disputes and breakups down the road. Ask them what they want and what they think they want. Ask them how they would handle different situations such as what would happen if something happened to them and they were no longer able or willing to go the educational route you set up for them. Your kids will have opinions on things that you didn't think they even thought about, and you'll find out all sorts of stuff about them including their needs and wants, as well as their ideas about your estate. By talking to your children before you sign your name to an estate plan, especially an irrevocable trust, you can do much to avoid angering them or creating rivalries between siblings after your death.

Most important, communicate before you die with *all* your heirs. And try to take the high road. Even if you have not spoken to a child in twenty years, or you disowned him or her because of past decisions you don't agree with, leave equal shares anyway. It will affirm your love and show that the child is equal to his or her other siblings, and it just may prompt the child to look at his or her own conduct and to take responsibility for his or her role in the situation.

Remember, the estate works when everyone works together. But the whole thing starts to fall apart when rivalries are set up. The dad who disowns his son may find that son coming back to challenge his estate. The best way to prevent this from happening is to communicate with all parties involved before you sign your name to anything.

Step Six: Providing for Disabled Children

If you have a disabled child, you have to do even more homework and even more planning. Any special-needs situation needs to be looked at and handled in the best and fairest way possible to all heirs. In this instance, you not only better have a plan, but you should plan with greater detail and oversight. You will also need greater input from all those affected by the decisions surrounding the disabled child. Plan the day-to-day care, the week-to-week care, and year-to-year care. Again I say, plan for the worst situation and pray for the best. Make sure there is a second person to oversee the personal representative's performance.

Step Seven: Charitable Giving

One option is that you give your money and assets to charity. In fact there are a lot of benefits to charitable giving. As I suggested earlier, if you have a lot of money, you can create your own foundation and even have your kids run it. Once money is in a foundation, it is not subject to estate taxes. You can offset tax obligations of your estate through charitable giving. Check with your tax advisors about when and how to give to the charity of your choice. They will guide you so that you can obtain the benefits of the gifts.

For trust and estate administrative purposes it gets tricky when you name too many charities as beneficiaries or name charities as contingent beneficiaries. (A contingent beneficiary is one that gets all or part of your assets because of an event that happens, such as: "If all my children die without issue, then all my money goes to X charity). Setting up a contingent beneficiary is fine, but know that if you name more than two, you've created an accounting nightmare. Whomever you name as a beneficiary, contingent or not, you've given them a right to demand accounting information of your trust—at the expense of the trust, of course. It can be costly because you have created a right which they will want to enforce. As a beneficiary, the charity has the right to monitor whether the event entitling it to its benefits is occurring, and it will always be in the lives of your children. By law, all beneficiaries have the right to talk to your trustee, demand information, receive accountings and reports, request tax information, demand information regarding management of assets, challenge decisions made by the trustee and so on. I once had a client who named ten charities in his trust, and while I admire his altruism, I had to honestly tell him that he allowed ten separate entities to invade his estate and his children's lives and create costly demands on the trust he created. I recommend two charities at most.

Step Eight: Familiarize Yourself with the Law

Before you begin writing there is another task you must complete. Get familiar with the laws surrounding your trust. Don't get me wrong; you can't possibly know all the trust law there is. Remember, it takes a law student an entire year of his three years of studying law to get familiar with estate law. However, I'm going to give you the basics. It's not easy reading, so be prepared. Get a good dictionary, and be ready to look up words with which you are not familiar. This is a vital step because part of my solution is for everyone to make informed decisions and that means knowing your rights. Make your lawyers, banks, and accountants inform you and advise you of the law. It will not only make them do the right thing, but they are an invaluable resource. Learn from them and then make decisions.

Our laws place boundaries around what is expected from individuals placed in positions of trust, and there are penalties imposed for those who stray from their obligation and duties. The law in California, similar to most states, requires that our trustees act solely in the interest of the beneficiaries, that they act impartially in investing and managing the trust property, taking into account differing interests of the beneficiaries, The trustee is prohibited from dealing with trust property for the trustee's own profit, and is obligated to preserve and make trust property productive, all in furtherance of the trust's purpose.

While these are the rules, the cost of enforcing them often exceeds the value of the trusts they are to protect. This makes the rules themselves unenforceable.

The Concept of Perfect Trust: The first thing to understand about the law is that if you set up a trust you should require the trustee to act on your and your beneficiary's behalf. This is the standard imposed on our trustees. It is called the "standard of care." The standard of care for a professional fiduciary is slightly more stringent than that imposed on a nonprofessional fiduciary (a relative, friend, family member, etc.). Nonetheless, the standard of performance and loyalty is very high. It is a standard of *absolute loyalty* where no action taken can be anything other than in the best interest of the person or entity represented.

The circuit judge in the case of *Ledbetter vs. First State Bank and Trust Company* stated it well:

> The foremost duty which a fiduciary owes to its beneficiary is undivided loyalty...If [the] trustee places itself in a position where its interests might conflict with the interests of the beneficiary, the law presumes that the trustee acted disloyally. It is not necessary for the beneficiary to show that the fiduciary acted in bad faith, gained advantage, fair or unfair, or that the beneficiary was harmed....

> As long as the confidential relation lasts, the trustee owes an undivided duty to the beneficiary under the trust, and cannot place himself in a position which would subject himself to conflicting duties, or expose him to the temptation of acting contrary to the best interests of the [beneficiary] ... The purpose of this rule is to require a trustee to maintain a position where his every act is above suspicion, and the trust estate, and it alone, can receive, not only his best services, but his unbiased and uninfluenced judgment. Whenever he acts otherwise, or when he has placed himself in a position that his personal interest has or may come in conflict with his duties as trustee, or the interests of the beneficiaries whom he represents, a court of equity never hesitates to remove him. In such circumstances the court does not stop to inquire whether the transaction complained of were fair or unfair, the inquiry stops when such relation is disclosed.[4]

---

4   Ledbetter vs. First State Bank and Trust Company (1996 11 cir) 144. SE.at 789

The Prudent Man Standard: What does it mean when the trustee manages our money and property? How does this duty of loyalty play out? Is this a guarantee that our trustees will not lose money placed in their care? No, not really! Take, for example, the dot-com bubble of the 1990s. Some companies were getting 20 percent returns-on-investment, and some trusts benefited greatly. But the question here is, should a 20 percent return on investment be the standard for our fiduciaries? Would a trustee not be loyal if their investments only returned 5 percent instead of 20 percent? Because the rules of loyalty are all over the lot, the courts recognized early that there was no way to judge whether one trustee was better serving his beneficiary than another and that we would never get anyone to act as trustee if saddled with a rigid standard that changed as the market changed. So back in 1830, in a case in Massachusetts called *Harvard College vs. Amory*[5], the Massachusetts Supreme Court held that:

> all that can be required of a trustee is that he conduct himself faithfully and exercise sound discretion and observe how men of prudence, discretion and intelligence manage their own affairs not in regard to speculation, but in regard to the permanent disposition of their funds, considering the probable income as well as the probable safety of the capital to be invested. [6]

This standard became known as the "Prudent Man Rule" and has since evolved into the "Prudent Investor Rule." (The Prudent Investor Rule also includes a series of other rules invoking the prudent man concept.) What this means in general is that the trustee has a duty to invest funds for the benefit of the beneficiaries,[7] taking into account their needs and circumstances. The trustee must "manage and invest the trust funds considering the purpose, terms, distribution requirements and other circumstances of the trust." The trustee's investment and

---

5   Harvard College v. Amory, 9 Pick. (26 Mass.) 446, 461 (1830)):

6   See, FN 12; see also www.peo7.com/htmFiles/PEOusLabor_Section264. htm-14k-

7   The trustee is governed by the Uniform Prudent Investor Act, which applies to most states and is governed by the local probate code, including sections 16045-16054 of the California Probate Code.

management decisions regarding the individual assets of the trust and the proposed course of action "must be evaluated not in isolation, but in the context of the trust portfolio as a whole and as a part of an overall investment strategy having risk and return objectives reasonably suited to the trust."[8] According to this standard, the trustee is lodged with the duty of putting together a plan for the beneficiaries taking into account the purpose of the trust and devising an investment strategy that will accomplish that purpose. For example, if the trust is established for the purpose of educating a child, and the child is five years old, a strategy must be established to meet the goal of educating the child through high school, college, graduate school, etc., depending upon the direction in the trust and availability of funds. Difficulty comes with differing standards of what constitutes "prudence."

The current Prudent Investor Rule is set out in the American Law Institute restatement of the Law Third, Trusts: Prudent Investor Rule, 1992,[9] which calls for sound diversification of assets, risk, and return based on the analysis by the fiduciary concerning the acceptable levels of risk appropriate to the purposes, distribution requirements, and other circumstances of the trust. The fiduciary is to avoid fees, transaction costs, and other expenses that are not justified by needs and objectives of the investment program. The trustee is to balance return and income while maintaining purchasing power.

Not surprisingly, the Prudent Man Standard is interpreted differently across the United States. So, too, the 1830 version of how a trustee should invest money has changed. The entire investment scene has evolved making the Prudent Man Standard even more difficult to apply. Today professional investors, money managers, trustees, and investment firms ascribe to what is called "Modern Portfolio Theory." Modern Portfolio Theory differs from simply choosing individual stocks and bonds in that investments are now described in terms of long-term-return rate and short-term volatility. The theory relies on

---

8   UPAIA; California Probate Code sections 16045-16054
9   § 227. General Standard of Prudent Investment: The trustee is under a
       duty to the beneficiaries to invest and manage the funds of the trust as
       a prudent investor would, in light of the purposes, terms, distribution
       requirements, and other circumstances of the trust.

economists who try to understand the market as a whole rather than relying on business analysts who try to determine what makes each individual investment unique. Volatility equals risk, and the analysis determines how much worse the downside of an investment can be in relation to the market average. The goal is always to find an acceptable level of risk and then to find a portfolio with the maximum expected return for the chosen level of risk. If this all sounds like voodoo to you, you are not alone. However, if you are a grantor, a trustee, or a beneficiary, it behooves you to take some time and learn about Modern Portfolio Theory of investment because it is the standard applied to investment of assets by your trust. For example, if you are a trustee and your beneficiary asks you why you did not follow Modern Portfolio Theory in the way you handled their trust, you better be able to respond why it was not used.

Uniform Trust Code: Because the rules applicable to trusts vary from state to state, there is a movement to standardize trust laws nationwide. Rules have been formulated in the "Uniform Trust Code" which is intended to provide consistency as well as provide rules where there are none. One of the key provisions of the Uniform Trust Code is that it adopts the Uniform Prudent Investor Act as a standard to be followed by trustees and proscribes that trust assets should be in diversified portfolios. It also sets damages for breach of fiduciary duty by the trustee and adds provisions for notifying beneficiaries of the existence of the trust when it becomes irrevocable.

Step Nine: Make an Estate Folder

It might seem obvious to say you should put everything that has to do with your estate plan—or at least copies of them—in one place. But many people have the various pieces of their estate scattered in various locations. As a result when it comes time to sort things out, papers are overlooked, missed, or even hidden making administration incomplete. Absent technology, set up a three-ring binder with tabs and pockets that holds everything important.

The main tabs you want to include are: inventory (which includes ownership documents and contracts); your will; your trust; your living will; all pertinent contact information; pre and post nuptial agreements, beneficiary information, asset inventory, mortgage and debt obligations, and miscellaneous.

The inventory will include all the photos and values of your material goods, copies of deeds and titles, prenuptial and postnuptial agreements (which should also be referenced in your will or trust), personal and business contracts, in short, anything that has to do with ownership. Put copies of all the important papers in the folder and have the originals in a safe-deposit box or other safe place because original documents can be altered.

The most current version of your will and your trust will include the name of your trustee, your beneficiaries, the division of your assets, as well as letters of instruction that include your goals and values and how you want your wishes carried out. I delve into these aspects in more depth in the next chapter. The living will should also be current, and by current, I recommend that you review your estate plan every three years, no matter how painful it may be. The more current your estate is at the time of your death, the more you can be sure that all will go according to your wishes.

You must include all important contact information for your beneficiaries, your trustee, your life insurance agent, your bank, your lawyer, and your accountant. In short, you need to include names, addresses, phone numbers, and e-mail addresses for everyone who will be connected to your estate both short term and long term. You also want to include usernames and passwords for all internet accounts so that the administrator can access important information as needed.

Step Ten: Start Drafting Your Plan

You've done your homework. You've gathered all the pertinent documents; you've talked to all the people involved. Now you can start planning your trust or will because you have information at your fingertips. You can now figure out how you can actually start planning out the design, implementation, and execution of your trust.

I began this book with a call for responsibility, and by taking the time to setup these three elements in your estate plan, you are well on your way to taking responsibility for your trust and making sure your plan works. To help you further, I'm now going to give you a basic outline of what needs to be in each of these three elements.

A. The Design Plan

The design of your trust or estate will dictate how decisions are made in the future. The goal here should not be to micromanage your personal representative but to give him/her/it boundaries within which to make decisions. Your goals will translate into a set of parameters for your trustee or executor to follow and provide a set of requirements for your beneficiaries to meet to receive the benefits. The best directives are meaningful but not so detailed they would constrict or smother the purpose of the trust or estate.

There should be minimum levels of constraints to guide our representatives in how we want them to implement our trust or estate. To the extent we relieve our personal representatives of the burden of making hard decisions about our funds, we can facilitate the administration, reduce the cost associated with making these decisions, and eliminate liability for our decision maker.

For both the will and the trust, each should address or have previously made decisions regarding the following ten items. These are not the only items that should be addressed, but I consider these the top ten:

1. Set forth the goal or purpose of your trust or estate.

2. Provide for accountability.

3. Provide for fiduciary liability.

4. Define the broad terms used in your trust or estate and have these terms correspond to the values you have set forth in a letter of instruction.

5. Test the financial model for your plan:
   - Have you properly funded your plan?
   - Have you established investment standards or norms?

6. Empower your beneficiaries.

7. Define the fees that are authorized.

8. Set priorities when there is a conflict, who prevails.

9. Provide a dispute resolution mechanism.

10. Provide for taxes.

B. The Implementation Plan

As I have pointed out before, here is where the proverbial "rubber hits the road" because it expresses how our wishes expressed in our design plan will be accomplished.

I have a confession to make here. I've been holding back a pertinent piece of information so that you could fully understand the effects of not having an implementation plan. The truth is, if you have a will, there are rules of administering your estate that must be followed. If you administered a trust in the same way you administered an estate through a will's probate process, you would be in good shape.

But there is a caveat to what I just said. While the will has specific procedural processes defined by statute as to how assets will be utilized and distributed, vigilance on the part of the beneficiaries with constant oversight must be in place for this system to work well. The same holds true for a trust; when you have a well-thought out implementation plan, the trust's goals are clearly linked to a process for accomplishing them rather than leaving them to the good graces of whomever we place in charge.

While I have gone into the many factors that work against ever accomplishing the goals of our trust, they are worth repeating. In a nutshell, our trust or estate plan is placed in an environment where competing interests, inattention, and misunderstanding all work to divert, misdirect, and frustrate our goals. In order to achieve our goals in this environment, we have to prepare an explicit plan that counteracts the environmental diversions and distractions that any trustee faces. In other words, we need an implementation plan.

The implementation plan is actually complementary to the trust document. It is contained either in letters of instruction or in a document stored in electronic form and it provides definitions of terms, values and goals of the grantor, directives as to how the terms are to be implemented on an asset by asset and/or beneficiary by beneficiary basis. It addresses at least the following basic issues:

- **Goals:** These include not only the main goals of the trust but goals as they relate to assets and/or specific beneficiaries. The implementation plan should address how the grantor envisions the assets will be utilized to reach the goals. This may include an investment profile and/or an articulated path as to how the grantor expects to accomplish the goals. The goals may be specific to each beneficiary or group of beneficiaries. The implementation plan should also address what happens to assets when goals are accomplished or frustrated.

- **Values:** Your values must be a prominent part of your trust. For example, if you value promoting self-support and independence in your beneficiaries, that should be articulated in your trust and letters of instruction. If you really do not want your children to be perpetual students, make sure you set out what you expect to accomplish by your trust.

- **Beneficiaries:** Give direction to your beneficiaries about what you expect of them and to the fiduciary that is to serve them. Your beneficiaries are part of your implementation plan, and they should know how you expect them to assist in the accomplishment of your goals. The plan should be transparent so they can keep it on track.

- **Priorities:** When there is a conflict between two interests, your plan will define who or what has priority.

- **Assets:** The plan should have directives for the particular assets of the trust. It should contemplate and address asset management, sale, division, apportionment, distribution, transfer, merger, assignment, allocation, termination, encumbrance, investment, etc. These directions may and even should be different for different assets.

- **Events:** The implementation plan anticipates predictable high- and low-probability events and provides boundaries for decision making when those events occur.

- **Disputes:** The plan anticipates disputes between beneficiaries, between beneficiaries and fiduciaries, and between co-fiduciaries. It either provides a procedure for their resolution or for a formal dispute-resolution mechanism.

- **Fees:** It addresses the fees to be paid to the personal representative. It may also provide a formal or informal process for fee approval, one that requires notice to beneficiaries and a forum for objection to fees before they are paid.

- **Conflicts of Interest:** The plan identifies potential and actual conflicts of interest and either has a no-tolerance policy or a clear resolution procedure for addressing conflicts.

Today, when an event occurs (for example: a request for distribution for the purchase of a car) the trustee goes to your trust document in the files and reads the trust to determine if there is any directive that indicates how to handle this particular request. Because the language of the trust and its organization do not allow for quick review, the terms may be missed, may conflict with other terms, or may be difficult to decipher. With no clear direction from the trust, the trustee looks to his/her/its own procedural manuals (if it is a professional trustee) and the law to direct decision making. In the absence of such direction, trustees will make it up as they go along based on experience or by simply doing the best they can. Lay trustees simply do what they think is best, whatever that is (and sometimes, unfortunately, that includes thinking that the money in the trust is theirs to distribute). Usually, it is the application of the trustee's own values that dominate at this point, not yours.

As trustees change, values change until there comes a time when you would probably not recognize the trust you set up. To prevent this and the host of other problems I named throughout this book, an implementation plan should include all of the below:

- Well articulated goals.
- The desired path on how to reach the goal.
- Sufficient funding so the goal can be accomplished.
- Well articulated values with parameters for asset distribution clearly defined in relation to those values.
- A standard against performance of the trustee can be measured
- A timeframe for performance.
- Markers that indicate performance or demonstrate a frustration of the goal.
- Reward for completion of the goal.
- A plan for the remaining assets when the goal has been accomplished.

Part of the follow-through on the implementation plan is creating a report card for compliance with the plan. It should be noted that most fiduciaries do an implementation plan, but it is largely aimed at meeting company policy and goals, not the goals of the grantor.

The implementation plan is dependent upon having someone willing to follow the directions given. Is there someone out there who will follow your wishes and do what you expect? It is better to find someone who can follow direction rather than someone who wants to do it their way? Meet with your personal representative to see if he/she/it will implement your plan in the manner and within the boundaries you have set. There may be some compromises made in finding a representative, and you may have to dovetail your plan with the processes and procedures that are compatible with theirs.

C. The Execution Plan

From the grantor's perspective, there is far less to do at this stage than in the earlier design and implementation stages of the trust or estate. The grantor can only try to assure that the implementation plan has an execution path in the real world so his/her goals can be accomplished.

Because trusts as they are currently set up do not have an execution plan except in the broadest of senses, it leaves a vacuum of information for the personal representative to fill in. This allows all sorts of oddities and even abuse. For example, say the trustee is a personal friend. The trust has no set time when disbursements are to be made, so the trustee sends the beneficiaries the money they're entitled to in a Christmas card. It looks like it is a gift instead of something that rightfully belongs to the beneficiary! Add to this the fact that the people we place in charge usually suffer from poor or no training, and it is not difficult to see that we must do a better job at all levels to assure that the tasks we have left are executed properly.

A well-designed trust linked to a well thought-out implementation plan will go a long way toward assuring the plan is executed in a manner contemplated by the grantor. And "execution" simply means that the check was cut on time; it went to the right location, for the right purpose; and there is follow-up oversight to assure that the funds were used for the intended purpose. Remember, the trust is a "disbursement vehicle." There may be precedent conditions for the disbursement, and you want to make sure that your trust is executed as contemplated by the trust. A trustee that fails to make the distributions at the time and in accordance with the terms and conditions of the trust instrument subjects him/her/itself to liability and frustrates the purpose of the trust.

The execution plan requires more than just a sophisticated calendaring system; it needs a system that tracks the event and required response with consistent oversight that the trust terms were followed, the goals furthered, and results documented. Does our current trust and estate system have this? Not really. What we have is an electronic calendar and checkbook that counts the money and tracks its path, and that is about it.

Both wills and trusts actually suffer from the lack of an execution plan. The execution path can be delayed and even derailed by a number of variables that interfere with the efficiency and efficacy of the legal framework designed to accomplish the goal of the estate. These variables come from any number of directions including: 1) procedural and process failures by the fiduciary (e.g. failure to follow the legal, procedural, tax, accounting, etc. rules which causes delay and added costs to the estate); 2) errors in judgment, mistakes, or intentional wrongdoings by the fiduciary (e.g. an intentional or unintentional diversion of funds to benefit the wrong person causes delay and a dissipation of funds); 3) unforeseen and unaddressed events (e.g. the intervening fire that destroys fiduciary records causes delays and dissipates estate funds).

Wills can also suffer from not having a well-integrated implementation and execution plan, and looking at the failures that occur from the perspective of a will can be instructive. The implementation of a will is set by statute and guides the administrator through the multiple steps necessary to value the assets, pay the debts and taxes, and distribute the assets to the beneficiaries. But at each stage there is the assumption that the executor of the will is making the right decisions to address each of these steps. For example, the failure of the executor to recognize that impending tax legislation could double the tax to the estate if a certain asset was not converted to a different form constitutes a failure of execution. Failure of execution can equally cripple an estate and cause losses to the beneficiaries.

These fundamental flaws in the administration of a will, despite court oversight, are only quadrupled in a trust where there is no oversight, implementation road, or execution path. Think about it. There are no real boundaries currently given for a trust's administration or decision making, and so they run an even greater risk than wills of going off the rails.

In the current system, the implementation and execution of a trust is set by the good graces of whomever we put in charge. There is no plan, there is no directive, there are no benchmarks for performance, and we rely on our trustees to self-validate their own actions. If our trustees were smart, they would follow probate rules. But how many do this? In our trusts, we actually place all of our trust in our trustees to handle our assets, make decisions for us, and do the right thing with no accountability for any of it.

Execution of your Directives: Since the execution of the trust is the nuts and bolts behind the design and implementation of your plan, there are some questions to ask yourself: "Do I have confidence that my plan is being executed properly?" and "If it goes awry, are there procedures in place to catch it and reclaim what was lost as well as get my trust back on track?"

The execution of your directives has to do with two very important elements: you and your trustee. You have to be able to ensure your trustee has documented decisions behind the transfer of funds and has the procedures in place to follow distributions. You want assurance that decisions have been made in compliance with the trust instrument in a timely and appropriate fashion, have been accounted for with confirmed receipts, and have been made in a manner consistent with fiduciary standards and laws. In order to ensure that all this happens smoothly, you need to make sure that:

1. Your personal representative has a set of reliable repeatable processes you can count on to work in the administration of your trust.

2. There are processes and procedures in place to reach the goals of the trust.

3. The cost of the execution plan is established.

4. You have accounted for the length of time that the task's execution should take.

5. There are processes in place to capture the decisions made.

6. Progress towards goals is measured by a definable standard.

7. The system is transparent to the beneficiaries so they can monitor performance

In order to ensure that these seven points run smoothly, it is important to ask yourself the following three questions in regards to the person you are considering to be your trustee: Is your personal representative accountable and auditable? Does your fiduciary possess the requisite skills to accomplish the goals you have set? Will they implement your plan with your values not theirs?

No matter how you set up your execution plan, the key words in any execution process are that the system should be consistent, efficient, and predictable. For a trust, there should be a process that is followed, either electronically or manually, when a request for distribution is made. It starts with a "trigger event" and moves through the process of granting or denying the request. The trigger event can be a request from a beneficiary, a directive from the trust, an outside event like a beneficiary turning eighteen and then entitled to benefits, or any number of other events that could trigger a distribution. Depending upon the event that triggers the distribution, the trustee must make sure that the benefit is to go to a valid, identified, and entitled beneficiary. This means that procedures are in place to assure that benefits go only to those entitled under the trust or by law at a time when benefits are to be paid. If, for example, the beneficiary requesting benefits is the child of an illegitimate heir, it must be determined whether the child is named as a beneficiary under the trust and entitled to benefits at the time requested.

The next step is to see if the trust document authorizes the distribution for the purpose and at the time requested. If benefits are contingent upon any action by the beneficiary or another condition, the trustee must notify the beneficiary of the condition precedent and that precedent condition must be satisfied before benefits may be made available. If all of the above steps are satisfied, the trustee has to determine two things: 1) are there funds available to meet the beneficiary request, and 2) are the funds in liquid form so they can be paid? If not, then a whole set of other procedures would go into effect in the sale of assets to meet the distribution request. Where all conditions and preconditions are met, a payment should be made without further condition.

Making the distribution does not complete the process however. There must be processes in place to monitor whether the payment is a one-time event or whether it will be duplicated, such as a payment of tuition for school. The check must be tracked. A properly set-up execution program ensures the check got to the school by requiring the school to sign a receipt of confirmation and return the receipt to the fiduciary. The check and disbursement would also go into the accounting system and be tracked for its deposit. This enables the trustee to keep accurate records as to the purpose, amount, and process of distribution, so it can be included in the quarterly report to the beneficiaries.

Right now, all of this work must be done manually. If this system were automated, it would take minutes instead of days to track such an event, and emerging technology will dramatically change what we may expect. However, until a dependable software program is made widely available, the execution of your trust will run the risk of being mired down in people who are ill-equipped and ill-prepared to administer it. Remember, the problems that plague trusts happen at all three stages—design, implementation, and execution. It is up to you to plan your trust so that when the time comes, your money and your assets go to those you intend to benefit.

CHAPTER 8

Handling Problems with Trustees and Beneficiaries

Chapter 7 outlined the steps you need to take to set up a trust that will ensure that your beneficiaries actually benefit from the trust. However, the overview doesn't help you address some of the specific problems that I have been addressing. In this chapter, I'm going to address the various problems that have to do with trustees and beneficiaries by offering you solutions. They are based on many years of handling trusts that don't work.

Picking the Right Trustee

While many trusts and estates seem to weather the difficulties of administration just fine and accomplish their intended purpose, there is nonetheless growing dissatisfaction among beneficiaries who complain that their trustee or estate representatives simply fail to do the job they were retained to perform.

In order to prevent the heartache and dissatisfaction, it is vital to choose the right trustee, but that is obviously no small task. There are many factors to consider when choosing a trustee, and before you sign anything, please carefully consider all that I'm about to tell you.

I have been surprised at the number of failed estates and trusts, unmet goals, lack of accountability, failure of assets, and arrogant appointed representatives who use trust funds to defend their fraudulent and negligent behavior. In order to ensure that this doesn't happen to you, make it easy for your personal representative whether a private fiduciary or a professional by providing a design and implementation plan they can follow. Providing this guidance in their decision making may save them from lawsuits in the handling of your trust and save your beneficiaries loss of assets.

Always remember that who we appoint may be making decisions for us before we die. This person may decide whether we stay at home, stay in a vegetative state or pull the plug. This is the person who will raise our minor children, run our companies when we are gone, and decide whether to sell off our assets. My recommendation for the best kind of trustee is actually splitting the duties.

Multiple Estate or Trust Representatives

Current fashion says that we name one person or entity as our personal representative with back-up successors named in sequence. Some people tell me they name their spouse because they are the closest to them. Others name their children, relatives, or friends. The problem with a personal trustee is that he or she will have to hire someone at the expense of the trust to guide them through the process of administration. Others have relatives who are doctors, lawyers, C.P.A.'s business people etc. who they think will better serve in this position than their more untrained relatives. The problem is most named representatives are not qualified for one or more of the roles in which we place them. They must serve as parent, investment/financial advisor, tax advisor, accountant, lawyer, and trust administrator.

I propose a better solution is to name different people for different roles. In my experience the combination of the professional and lay trustee with defined roles, duties, and obligations has served as the better model for trust administration. If you can, have three co-fiduciaries, a combination of two family members with at least one beneficiary and one professional. This establishes a more accountable model. Another variation of this is where you name one lay representative, one beneficiary, and one professional. Both these combinations have worked well for some because three trustees provide checks and balances and overall supervisory authority for the others.

No matter what combination you choose, you should provide that two of the co-trustees should be able to outvote the third trustee. This creates an alignment of interests and motives to get the job done.

For the "parental role" while children are still minors, choose someone different than the person who manages the assets with each keeping tabs and crosschecking the other. This will likely require that you select a dispute-resolution mechanism as well. The professional fiduciary best fills the role of financial and asset manager as this is a typical service they provide. This is not to say that the professional fiduciary should be left to its own devices to determine the investment scheme for your trust. They should not. If you have put together a good design plan, you will have set the parameters for your financial goals and investment plan. You will have provided the fiduciary with enough direction in the design and implementation plans that they do not have to guess at how they are to accomplish the goals you have set.

The area of parental role is best served by someone who the beneficiaries love and trust. If you have children to raise and nurture, the professional fiduciary is usually not the best choice. Family members may serve in this role and should have input into the financial decisions made for the minor or special-needs beneficiary. Hence a designed working relationship between the family member and the professional should be structured for accountability and for maximum benefit to the beneficiaries.

The non-family-member lay-administrator may also contribute. If there is a professional who knows your family and who you trust like an accountant, lawyer, financial manager etc. (again remember this is not the person who wrote the trust) the background they bring to facilitating the administration of your trust can be valuable. Again the checks and balances among all three people provide a mechanism to assure that decisions are not made unilaterally. The multiple parties generally allow safeguards to be put in place against the self-validation of decision making when only one trustee serves.

No matter whom you choose as your trustee, put language in your trust allowing your beneficiary to remove a poorly performing trustee. Do not lock your heirs in for life to a trustee who just siphons off fees and assets over time. Make your trustee accountable to your beneficiaries. The trustee should be working for your trust and be accountable to your beneficiaries for their performance. Put language in that assures that there is accountability, and that decisions behind the numbers are disclosed to your heirs.

On the subject of language, it is also important to eliminate language that can be used against your beneficiaries. It is there simply to protect the trustee's position. For example there is a "no-contest" term commonly found in today's trusts. They usually read similar to the following:

If any person contests or opposes this trust or its terms in any manner directly or indirectly, in whole or in part, or attempts to succeed to any portion of my trust other than through the terms authorized by this trust such person shall take nothing from my trust as set forth herein, and any gift herein to which such person would otherwise be entitled shall be revoked, rendered void and shall pass to those persons who would be entitled thereto as if the contesting person has predeceased me.

The intended purpose of this provision is to assure that the wishes of the grantor are honored and unintended beneficiaries are not allowed to usurp the trust and its terms. A noble goal. *But*, I have seen errant fiduciaries who may have mismanaged the assets of the trust use these terms to defend themselves. The fiduciary may threaten beneficiaries who challenge their "judgment" with disinheritance. At the very least, I would take out the language *"in any manner directly or indirectly,"* thus limiting opposition to the trust.

When you name multiple trustees, above all, make sure to define the roles you expect each to play. For example, if you had a minor and used the multiple trustee scenario I recommend, the parental role of raising your child would overlap into the investment role as both surrogate parent and investment advisor must interact to meet and plan for the needs of the child, Each would have specific tasks; the surrogate parent would deal with the day-to-day feeding, housing, and educating the child while the investment advisor would be planning how the funds of the trust can pay for all of it. But each role requires interaction with the other. The third trustee in this scenario may simply be one who oversees the performance of the two and takes care of the reporting and accounting function. All three working together can assure that the goals of maintenance and education are met.

Anticipate events; set goals and limit decision making by your fiduciary by addressing the issues before they have to; set limits of time and money as to how long and how much you authorize to be spent on reaching a goal; plan for frustration or failure of goals and create a plan B. Fees should be geared to hours spent not percentage of assets under management.

Questions for the Professional Fiduciary

While you should be able to name whomever and however many people you want to administer your trust, you may be placed in a situation where you only have the option of a professional fiduciary. If that is the case, get answers to the following questions when evaluating whether to select one trustee over another (Really, if you have a professional fiduciary in any capacity, you should have them answer the following):

- Does the fiduciary provide annual accountings to the beneficiaries?
- Is the accounting in a form consistent with applicable law?
- Does the fiduciary prepare a narrative written report (not just in numbers) explaining the actions taken and decisions made on behalf of the trust?
- How do they work with the beneficiaries to meet their needs?
- What fees are charged for their services and what services are actually provided for the amounts paid? Is the fee schedule subject to change? Get the entire fee schedule, add it up, and see whether your trust can afford to lose that amount annually.
- Does your fiduciary put together a plan to meet the goals you have set and do you as grantor agree with the plan? Are there benchmarks of performance set so your beneficiaries can tell whether the goal is being met?

- Will the fiduciary follow the directions you have left and implement the plan as you anticipate?
- Does the trustee want waivers to be signed relieving them of liability for negligence in their administration requiring a gross-negligence standard before recovery by your beneficiary as a condition for accepting the trust?
- Does the trustee want to be relieved from the liability for reviewing the conduct of the former trustee? (You should *not* relieve them of this obligation.)

Is the decision-making process transparent? Are there processes in place upon which the beneficiaries can rely that are predictable and consistent? Are decisions made by committee? (You want to avoid the committee if you can. While professional fiduciaries often utilize "trust committees" for decision making, they tend to be unidentifiable, unaccountable, and non-responsive bodies utilized to obstruct access to benefits.) To get the specialized service that everyone desires, it is important to break the mold. Administering a trust is a tough job, and it helps, not hinders, a trust to have multiple people handling the multiple tasks a trust requires.

Establish Guidance for Your Trustee

It is up to the grantor to direct and instruct the trustee in the manner of his or her administration. The trust document should be clear as to exactly what the trustee is expected to do. Parameters should be set for administration within set boundaries for decision making. Assets should be divided between beneficiaries so as to avoid infighting and claims of more benefits to one beneficiary over another.

Where there are multiple beneficiaries and one pot of undivided assets, structure a division on paper with a proportionate share going to each. Where one beneficiary requires more than others make sure that the invasion of trust funds takes only the proportionate share of the requesting beneficiary and does not dissipate another beneficiaries' share of assets.

Create a Better Model of Administration

While the best solution to most trustee problems starts with a team of representatives, matched to their most obvious roles, it is vital to empower your team with good directions in the form of the design, implementation, and execution plans. This combination of the best team, with clear direction, expectations, and a good operating process will greatly increase your chances of successfully meeting the goals of your estate.

The first and most important point in administration of a trust is its language. Do not grant broad authority or broad discretionary powers to any of your trustees to do as they deem appropriate. Make sure that the terms you use are consistent and that they are defined clearly and have standards against which performance can be measured. Any existing trust should be restructured to meet these standards as well.

Most important, ask your fiduciary about their capabilities, whether they can provide on-demand accountings, reports of decisions made, streamlined and predictable distributions, tracking of assets and investments, and fee reduction based on automated systems. Here you want to start looking at the balance of interests in the administration of your trust. The beneficiary's interests may not align with the interests of the trustees and hence there is a risk of loss to your trust. This delicate balance of decision making should be weighted in

> **Technology Teaser**
> Technology in this area will provide the grantor with decision-making capability for the future and he/she will be able to set parameters for their personal representative.
>
> Technology will facilitate and automate much of the administrative process so your trust or estate is administered within predictable boundaries set by you. Your beneficiaries will rely on the implementation plan you have established rather than on the discretion of your personal representative.
>
> Technology will also help your fiduciary increase their reporting capabilities. They can provide on-demand accountings, reports of decisions made, streamlined and predictable distributions, tracking of assets and investments and fee reduction based on automated services.
>
> The benefit to all is it will allow the fiduciary the capability to address problems as they arise with immediate turn around because the grantor has already facilitated this process by projecting himself into the future.

favor of the beneficiaries who continue to bear the most risk in the administration of the trust.

Clearly set up, requirements of accountability, transparency, repeatable processes, access to benefits, and information regarding decision making. You also want to require predictability for distributions. All this information should be available at any time. If these plans are in place, the risk of loss to your trust and to the fiduciary are reduced. Reduced risk equates to more efficiency, lower cost, more predictability, and a preservation of assets with increased service to your beneficiaries.

It is important if you already have written a will or a trust to revisit it and look for terms that could be interpreted in a manner different from your intent. It is also important that you understand the documents that have been drafted on your behalf. If you don't understand them how will your family understand what you intended? It is vital that you supply definitions that accompany a trust or will to assist in its interpretation. The definitions should either be in the trust or will or contained in letters of instruction. However, definitions are just the beginning in setting parameters for administering the terms of your trust or will. Boundaries must be spelled out defining what decisions may be made, how your instructions are to be implemented, and guidance on their execution. I can't say this enough: how a trustee implements or accomplishes your goals are as important as the goals themselves.

Create Priorities for your Trustee or Administrator to Follow

A plan that works involves more than just a grant of funds or a gift of particular assets. Understanding the process of how gifts are prioritized is important too. Often the gifts are tied up for years in probate or trust, depending upon a variety of road blocks to their distribution simply because the grantor did not know or anticipate the process that blocked the distribution.

When a conflict arises in the form of competing demands for the same funds, make sure you have a resolution process in place. This is in the form of priorities. For example health demands may have priority over educational demands. The surviving spouse may require support but the beneficiaries want distributions that cut into that support. Is there a process in place to resolve these conflicting claims?

Anticipate the Cost of Administration

Before you give your property away or attempt to bestow a gift:

- Make sure you have the resources available to meet the: estate-tax, attorney's fees, appraisers, auction fees, trustees, accountants, litigation costs, and court costs.
- Analyze your assets, know their value, tax liability, debt, and creditor's claims; designate which assets are to be sold to meet it all.
- Anticipate medical and funeral costs.

In other words, establish how you intend to pay for it all so these items do not block the ultimate distribution to your heirs.

Set Standards of Accountability that are Loud and Clear

The standards you set in your trust or will should be the highest standards that exist in law, period. If the person is not adept at trust and estate management, anticipate the cost of training them or hiring an expert to help them.

As I have said many times before, it is important to contemplate the worst in planning your estate. I am talking about the person you place in charge of your assets taking everything, diverting, or losing your assets so your heirs never see them. Although we do not pay attention to the numerous news articles about errant trustees absconding with funds of the trusts they manage, we should. It happens more often than we would like to acknowledge.

Sometimes, the loss is more subtle; the trustee may funnel assets into instruments or investments that just by chance benefit themselves, or money is siphoned off in fees, charges, and losses. The beneficiaries are the losers. It is important to set a standard for your trustee to operate within. Again parameters can be set in letters of instruction for investment, asset management, etc. Make sure the trustee is responsive to your beneficiaries and allows access to information and decision-making. The secret decisions behind closed doors where benefits are just denied with no explanation is not a standard you want to promote.

Handling Beneficiaries

The beneficiaries should be the ultimate winners in your trust. It is for them you have planned in the first place. You worked hard for your money and you want your heirs to reap the benefits of what you have left behind. In order to ensure that happens, here are my suggestions:

Define Beneficiaries

First and foremost, define who you want to benefit. Identify your beneficiaries with as much detail as you can e.g. social security number, driver's license number, phone number, last address, and full name and other names known by. Also define the people you do not want to benefit, e.g. unknown illegitimate children, stepchildren, an ex-spouse, etc. If a beneficiary cannot be found, your trust must pay for private-investigator fees and tracing agencies to locate them. Ultimately the gift may be deemed abandoned and revert to the residuary clause of the instrument and pass to others. Avoid this problem by getting it right and updating the information regularly.

If there are to be restrictions on the gift, define them. Perhaps the beneficiary is a minor child. This triggers a series of court proceedings for the protection of the child. Someone must be formally appointed the guardian to receive benefits in the child's name. If you have minor children, make sure the guardianship is under court supervision so that the funds or gift are protected and the court supervises the distribution to the intended beneficiary, not the person in charge of the funds. The court oversees the maintenance of the gift for the child until the child reaches eighteen. When the child reaches eighteen, the court will no longer supervise the funds. At this point, set up a mechanism so there is oversight and help to your eighteen year old.

Set parameters for care and investment for your family and assets. Do not leave your family or personal representative in the dark as to exactly what you want. Be clear about what investments you think are sound. Provide parameters for investment designed to meet your goals.

Define the Goals for the Beneficiary

What you want to accomplish with a trust varies from family to family, but there are some common goals that are relatively universal. Certainly the goal of the trust should reflect the values that you hold and provide incentives for self-sufficiency and self-actualization for your beneficiaries. The best trusts provide a culture or philosophy for the family that the grantor wants to promote. After all your trust may be touching several generations and the values that you establish in the formation of the trust should be thought through and reflected in the benefits that are granted. If you value education, this value should be reflected in what you will fund with your trust. If you value community service and giving back, this philosophy should be instilled in the language of and implementation plan of your trust. If you want to promote self-reliance your trust would be structured with incentives to promote this. Expanding upon what I outlined earlier the reasons people create trusts vary from support, education, health, special needs, charity, taxes, financial supervision, preservation of assets, promotion of self-sufficiency etc.

As always, each of the above-listed goals should be defined further and linked to a plan of implementation so that both the beneficiary and the trustee are well informed and the interpretation of goals and desires of the grantor are not left to the discretion of the personal representative.

Set Standards that Apply to Each Beneficiary

Just as there should be a clearly defined plan for your administrators, there should be an administration plan for your beneficiaries. They should be made aware of the parameters that apply to the use of the trust's fund. They should know what the trust will pay for in terms of education, welfare, support or the myriad of other terms the grantor sets forth in the trust. If you're dealing with education benefits, for example, the beneficiary should be aware if you authorize not only tuition and housing, but all the peripherals like meal plans, furniture for the apartment, cable lines for their computer, wireless phone service, and parking. They should also be aware of how many years of college will the trust pay for or if you have made the benefits from the trust conditional upon graduating within a certain number of years. If you want your grandchildren to be provided for, the parents should be well aware of the contribution they are expected to make as well. In order for the trust to be executed smoothly, the beneficiary—as well as the trustee—should know what to expect.

We must recognize that the strings we place on assets also bind the person we want to benefit. Conditions for receipt of benefits should be simple and limited. Recognize that the individual beneficiary wants to be treated with a level of respect for his or her own wishes and that the benefit should be exactly that, not a strangle-hold on the person.

How Do You Divide Your Assets?

Most of us do not have assets that can be split in two, three, or four parts easily unless the asset is sold and the funds are divided between the heirs. But what about the family bible, the parents wedding or engagement ring, the heirloom oriental rug, or the painting in Dad's den? Perhaps more difficult is the division of real property. It is rare to find two equally situated and valued pieces of property.

For personal property, it is important to list it. As I advised you in chapter 7, if you have an inventory of what you have with a relative value assigned to each item, you will have saved your personal representative hours of work and provided yourself with the opportunity to get input from your heirs or beneficiaries as to what they want. At least with this process you have something to work from. Your heirs can identify items that they would like. Knowing what each would prefer gives you the power to designate the gift and to equalize the division before death. You may simply choose to make specific gifts of the items before your death and save your estate from paying estate tax on the item.

The division of real property can also be problematic. In one estate, in an effort to treat their children equally, the parents had two pieces of real estate at relatively the same value. They gave one property to one child and the other to the second child. But at the time of death, the properties were not of equal value. One was located at a site closer to a marginal area while the other enjoyed a more favorable location. One of the heirs benefited to a greater extent than the other and always resented the inequality. The solution, while not perfect, would have been to give each child an undivided one-half interest in each property, or give one property to each but reconcile the fairness through a differential split of the liquid assets upon death.

The best laid plans can also take a turn. I saw one case where the parents had three daughters. They had a vacation home at the beach and left the children each a one-third interest in the home. On the parents' deaths, one of the daughters did not want an interest in the home and allowed one of her sisters to buy her out. The daughter with a two-thirds share told the remaining sister she was allowed only one-third of the time at the house. This family is still in dispute. The parents made a good decision but did not anticipate the potential play out of events. Had they discussed the issue with their children, they would have learned that one of their daughters did not want an interest in the house and could have structured their estate accordingly. In another instance the parents spent funds sending one child through college and then medical school while the other child pursued a less-costly career in design. The child who had not received the benefit of the graduate school education through medical school expected her parents to give her either through inheritance or a direct gift an amount equal to the amount spent by them on her sibling's education. Had the parents thought about this eventuality, they could have planned in a manner to equalize the children and perhaps could have avoided the resulting conflict.

But perhaps this is too simplistic. An equal division simply takes the parents out of or reduces the chances that they will be "blamed" for the disputes that arise. It does not solve years of sibling rivalry that may continue no matter what is done. So too where there is a blended family, equality of gifts does not work. Whatever was owned by the respective parent before marriage should go to the children of that earlier marriage. What is earned or acquired during the second or subsequent marriage can be divided up equally but once again efforts to communicate the issues to the parties should be undertaken for the best result.

Equal Division of Assets of the Trust

As you start planning the division of assets in your trust, you might think that it is a question of whether you can benefit one beneficiary over another. However, I find that the real question is whether you should. Equality does not always result in family unity, but I find that some sort of equality of gifts to children has a way of neutralizing bad feelings between parent and child and between siblings. While it may not take out the rivalries from the past, at least it does not become a new issue from which disputes can arise. Having had to deal with trust cases from the administrative side, I can say without reservation that there is *nothing* more divisive than inequality of gifts among children of the same parents. If there were jealousies or rivalries before death, these rivalries explode into disputes at death.

Many a grantor has expressed the view that they will no longer be around when their trust goes into effect, so they do not care what their children think. But the reality is that we do care. If we have been any kind of parent, we have tried to foster family unity, a sense of caring for one another, and a genuine respect for each other as a unique individual worthy of our love, respect, and support. It certainly is not our goal to perpetuate problems if we can avoid them.

There are of course those situations where one child has received more help from their parents than their more capable siblings. In this regard it should be understood that each child may go through the process of tallying up in his or her own mind what was done for each of them. If the tallying results in an inequity between children, again bitterness and anger bubble to the surface. At one Christmas, I was surprised to learn that my children had tallied up the cost of their gifts to determine whether they had received an equal amount. In another instance, parents were confronted by their son who went to public school and complained that his sister had been allowed a private-school education. While other things were done for the son including tutors and a car, the son still expressed resentment for what he perceived as unequal treatment.

I find that the key to any bequest is communication. Talk to your children about what you want to do and get their reaction. If you think one of your children needs more help than the others, discuss what you can do. Even if all the children do not agree, they will recognize that it is your money and assets to do with as you please, and they have been advised of your feelings and intentions. This alone may limit internal family hostilities.

While I advocate the equal division of assets, I do recognize that for a variety of reasons you may decide that equal is not appropriate for your family. It is important to recognize that your views in this regard may change over time as the circumstances of your children and heirs may change. If for example one of your children is a chronic drug addict, you may choose to focus your wealth on the more productive members of your line and leave the drug addict nothing, anticipating that the funds would simply be squandered feeding the addiction. Yet you should also entertain the notion that your errant child may not always suffer the stigma of addiction and that he or she may indeed find his or her way out from under it and then struggle to survive. Drafting a will or trust should never be an all-or-nothing proposition as there are means of providing incentives for better behavior. A bequest or share of the trust can always be conditioned upon proof of freedom from the addiction—e.g. if the person receives a clean medical clearance similar to that imposed on our athletes for a period of two years, is tested randomly over that two-year period and comes out clean, then 20 percent or less of the funds of his or her bequest could be released to him or her. Over the next two years the same process is employed. If the person is clean for a ten-year period, then a larger bequest could be granted. Similar restrictions can be implemented requiring the person to prove employment. You can have the trust match the funds earned over a designated period of time.

Since I tend to believe that there should be an opportunity for redemption and cleaning up one's act, I also believe that there should be a period allotted to the disinherited person to attain the gift if certain conditions are fulfilled. The choice then shifts to the beneficiary who either undertakes the effort to obtain the gift or forfeits it to other heirs by reason of his or her own default. But the choice is theirs, and that is key.

An unequal share may certainly be appropriate where there is a permanent disability suffered by one child. The need is greater and the siblings should understand that you are taking care of the problem so they do not have to. Communicate this to your children and explain why their share will be less than their disabled sibling's. In most instances it is the communication that makes the situation understandable and ultimately forecloses disputes and resentments.

Take the time to look at any issue from your children's perspective and balance the competing interests between them if you can. Efforts made after death via a will or a trust to equalize your children through different gifts tends not to work. These efforts are usually unsuccessful because the gifts tend not to be equal. For example, a gift during the grantor's lifetime of $25,000 for graduate school is not equal to a $25,000 gift to the other sibling on the death of the parents ten years later. The earlier gift afforded the child the opportunity to go to graduate school while the same amount ten years later could not grant the sibling the same opportunity.

There are those who argue that they have limited resources. Some of their children are brighter than others and they want to give their money to the children who have the greatest potential for maximizing the benefit from the limited resources. For example, parents may want to benefit their son because they know he will actually go to college and complete a degree while his sister may have little motivation and few skills. The parents are certain that the funds will be squandered by their daughter while their son will have to support a family. The reality is there is no crystal ball, and it would be better to discuss with each child what you are thinking and how you value industrious efforts. Faced with being disinherited, the daughter may prove the parents wrong by enrolling in college herself. It is a mistake to assume that one will remain the low producer for one's entire life.

The conditional gift based on performance and milestones where the gift defaults to the other sibling or a charity if progress is not met provides at least monetary incentive to actually attain a level of productivity and proficiency. If the beneficiaries understand the thinking behind the gift, they have the opportunity to change your mind or prove you wrong. After death it is too late to do either.

If you find yourself in a situation where you have not made the most prudent decisions regarding the equality of your children, try to solve the problem as soon as possible. If necessary hire a family mediator or counselor and explain what you are trying to accomplish. Explain to your children that the inequity was not intended. It is not a reflection of favoritism but a reflection of the best you could do at the time.

Cultural differences and prejudices also may dictate inequality. To this end the family may accept the outcome and anticipate it. Communication about prejudices, cultural expectations, and family values should be shared. Often the children are not aware of the full impact their parent's beliefs may have on them. Nor do the parents always consider the impact of the provisions of their trusts and estates on their children. I sometimes see children equalizing the estate after death where their parents failed to do so. This neutralized the bad feelings engendered by the parent's decisions.

I admit, some situations are more of a challenge than others and no matter how hard you try to promote feelings of unity and love, things do not always play out as anticipated. In my experience situations that require more care, planning and work include but are not limited to: 1) blended families with children from more than one marriage; 2) families that include adopted or foster children; 3) same-sex relationships; 4) illegitimate children; 5) high-net-worth individuals with significant assets; 6) special-needs situations; 7) families that already exhibit hostility and dysfunction toward each other. Where any of these situations exist, greater effort in designing the estate plan is warranted. And as always, whether your estate plan succeeds or dissolves into expensive acrimonious litigation in large part depends upon the time and energy you have devoted to the plan itself. If you have anticipated events, thought about each asset and its disposition, contemplated rivalries and jealousies, resolved issues and thoroughly planned for each beneficiary, you will go a long way toward establishing a plan that works.

Can You Control Behavior through Your Gifts?

What this all comes down to is whether or not you can control behavior through your gifts. The answer to that is a resounding yes, but will that control of behavior last? Probably not. The real question here is, what control do you want to have? Here is the rub. Money can be a blessing and a curse. While we all want our children to become happy, healthy, self-supporting individuals, yet unwittingly we may set in motion the very opposite effect through our estate plan or trust.

Promote Behavior You Want

Your trust should reward behavior and goals that you want to promote and discourage behavior you disapprove of. Take for example this sentence: "The trust shall provide for the education of the beneficiary for so long as the beneficiary remains in college but in no event longer than five years or the attainment of a bachelors degree whichever occurs first." This clearly specifies five years of education to attain a bachelor's degree. After five years there is no further funding. The benefits, time period, and expectations are defined. However, while this works as a limited provision, as I've noted before, it requires other definitions as to exactly what is included in the term "education."

The conditions of a trust or will that seem to motivate and work the best are the ones that specifically lay out the goal, the path to achievement, and the period within which the goal is to be accomplished. Receipt of benefits is directly linked to performance, and failure of performance equates to a failure of benefits. Tie distribution to goals like graduation, first job, or promotions. Reward events which you approve, e.g. marriage, success in a new business, children, or any other event that fits into your values and goals.

Benefits should be as predictable as possible. Do not leave your beneficiaries to beg for benefits which are in the discretion of your trustee.

Cultural Preferences and Preferential Treatment

I mentioned earlier that cultural traditions and expectations can come into play when you're thinking about dividing your assets. Cultural expectations can play a huge role in your trust, but I advise to proceed with caution.

America is the great melting pot for immigrants from all over the world. Each has brought their own belief systems, family, religion, and traditions, and each may want to perpetuate those cultures and religious beliefs here in America. Our laws, applicable to trusts and wills, allow perhaps the broadest boundaries within which to pass those cultural traditions on to the next generation. We are given freedom of expression and in only a few instances do our courts interpret the provisions of the trusts or wills to be so out of line with standards of society that they will not be upheld. For example a provision that gives funds to the daughter only if she marries a certain race would not be upheld; it would simply be struck down as unconstitutional. Yet provisions that provide for the funding of the education of a child only if he or she attends a particular religious school will usually be upheld. After all, it is the grantor's money and if he or she wishes to promote a certain belief system or conduct, then the grantor is free to do so.

While it is good to educate your children in their history and culture, it is important to understand the difference between passing on traditions and passing on discrimination and other beliefs that may cause family division and resentment. An Asian professor at a large university told me that he and his brother were co-trustees of the family trust and that they had no problems as they got along and agreed on the actions taken for the trust. I asked him if he and his brother were the only beneficiaries and if their father's estate had been divided equally between the two of them. He said he had two sisters who did not receive an equal share and that he and his brother received the same larger share. He said their father favored the male children. I asked if he still enjoyed a good relationship with his sisters. He admitted sheepishly no. His sisters resented the fact that they had not received an equal share and resented even more the fact that the two brothers controlled their funds. He said that his sister's children did not play with his or his brother's children and that the relationship was strained to nonexistent. Nonetheless, the man expressed satisfaction that his sisters could do nothing about the inequity. In another family, culture dictated that the first-born male received the majority of the inheritance and the younger brothers receive a disproportionate lesser share. The daughters received nothing as it was expected that they would marry and their husbands provide for them. I'm sure you can guess what happened to this family when that trust went into effect.

I would urge caution with respect to cultural dictates. While they are important and define who we are, some can be damaging. It is also important not to assume that the dictates of the past will necessarily play out in the future. The daughters may never marry and be left with nothing. Yes, it is your money. You can leave it to whomever you choose, but will your legacy promote family unity or family resentment? The decisions you make with respect to your trust can be divisive to the point of promoting hatred or they can be thoughtful, promoting family unity.

Knowing all the players and feelings of each can help you make better decisions. Place yourself in the shoes of the beneficiaries and see if you would appreciate the gift and how it was structured. How would *you* react to the gift(s) you propose to give if you received them from your parents? Can you anticipate a problem? If so you may want to rethink the structure of your gift. If you strive to be fair, it may not always be perceived as such by the people who are the recipients of the gifts. Again, it is worth communicating with your beneficiaries and finding out their views about an intended bequest or inheritance before it is set in stone.

Be Practical About What you Can Afford

Our greatest desire may be to benefit our friends and family so their lives are easier than ours. Yet our wish list must recognize and be designed to deal with reality. No matter how you choose to divide your assets and no matter what restriction you place on their distribution, make sure that the trust can meet its financial demands. Our own care may dissipate the gift we intended for our beneficiaries. We are all living longer, and we should anticipate that we might not have enough to get our grandchildren through college. If you do not have the funds to pay for college, set aside a fund for contribution to college or simply a gift to be utilized as the beneficiary sees fit.

Dispute Resolution Mechanism

The hard truth remains that no matter how well you plan, circumstances change and unforeseen events occur. So above all, your trust or will should provide a method for resolving disputes. Assets should be valued and a procedure instituted to determine who is to choose from the assets first with alternating choices until the assets are all divided. The assets should be grouped into asset groups of relatively equal value so the choices made are consistent with a true division. If an impasse is hit, the will or trust should spell out a methodology for resolving disputes. It can be as simple as flipping a coin or as complicated as formal mediation or litigation; it is your choice. But remember the more difficult the process, the more likely the process will consume the value of the assets in dispute.

Enforcing the Rules

While the law provides mechanisms and rules that govern our fiduciaries, the enforcement of those rules is a daunting task. First the beneficiary must recognize that there is a breach for which there is a remedy at law. If the beneficiary is not a lawyer trained in trust and estate law, he or she may not recognize that the conduct of his or her trustee or executor is actionable. Because all records are maintained by the fiduciary and the beneficiary may not have the complete picture, the beneficiary may not discover error or wrongdoing until the loss has already occurred. Once the breach is discovered the beneficiary's sole remedy, short of voluntary correction by the errant fiduciary, is a lawsuit. This involves hiring attorneys, preparing pleadings, and a court battle. These battles tend to take years. Since the trustee or estate administrator can use money from the estate or trust to defend against the challenge, the cure can often cost more than the ailment. Hence prevention is a better solution. But prevention requires vigilance and a plan that can be enforced without litigation.

Where the rules are defined and are recognized by all as the method and means of taking care of the particular estate or trust, and the beneficiaries are on top of the information they receive with sufficient understanding of what they are to look for, errors are minimized. It is the fog of language with broad undefined boundaries of conduct that create the problems.

CHAPTER NINE
Defining Values

Throughout this entire book, I have been admonishing you to define as clearly as you can your values and goals for your trust. I've been telling you that if you don't have your values specifically spelled out either in the trust document itself or in letters of instruction, your trustee can make decisions regarding your funds that wouldn't necessarily agree with yours. Without guidance, they can invest the money in your trust in ways you wouldn't agree with—or are even morally opposed to. They can distribute, or not, the funds in your trust in ways that don't conform to your wishes. However, I have yet to give you any specific direction on how to define your values in a trust.

How to go about defining your values is the thrust of this chapter, and while it is the shortest one in the book, in many ways it is the most valuable because this is the one area that the whole trust industry has patently failed to address. What the industry fails to deal with is the fact that the only real way you can clearly define an administration plan for your trustees to follow and your beneficiaries to be happy with is to have some way of defining your values. Once your values have been define, you can then clearly outline how you want the goals of your trust to be accomplished within those defined values.

A trust ultimately projects your legacy of values to your heirs. A trust actually provides a unique opportunity to think about and define what your values really are and what message you want to leave with the gifts you have given. For the overall goal of any trust is to discern how the grantor's values are defined in the context of the world he or she knows and then to apply those values into the world in which the grantor's heirs will live. The values must be flexible as they may bend and change with time and circumstance, and yet they must be forever consistent so as to provide a basis for reliance and trustworthiness.

Values Travel

If you want to have your values followed, they must be defined in terms that can travel and survive from generation to generation. And remember, you are setting boundaries not giving definitions. Definitions alone are insufficient. Take the broad category of health as an example. First you need to define what you mean by "health." Do you value good health? Do you want your money spent on preventative health care such as dental care, regular doctor's visits, addressing illness early, regular exercise, etc? Or do you see health care as acute care only? If you do, that is something you want to articulate so that your trustee can make decisions

> **Technology Teaser**
> In the new trust technology, there will be a series of value definitions to choose from. Your choice of what you mean by "health," for example, will in turn define if, when, and what benefits your beneficiaries will receive in response to a request for health benefits.

based on how you feel about health benefits. You also have to consider what your trust is intended to accomplish. It may not be intended as a support system but an emergency reserve for times of real need.

You want to make it clear to your trustee and beneficiaries whether the trust will pay for health insurance, emergency care, or preventative care, and they also need to know the limitations if any of these benefits. What you write will in turn define if, when, and what benefits your beneficiaries will receive. So no matter who is administering your trust and no matter how long the trust is in effect, if you have outlined your values, your trustee has boundaries for his/her decision making.

Values Help Determine Priority

The general areas trusts typically encompass are "health," "education," "welfare," "support," "maintenance," "standard of living," "well-being," "standard of care," and even "care"—in other words, all the words that are open to definition and abuse. However, I find that problems and disputes arise not only because of lack of definition but because these areas often overlap each other. Take the two terms "maintenance" and "standard of living." Oftentimes, competing interests of the beneficiaries can make for nightmarish decisions by the trustee. Here's one of my favorite examples. The assets in question are a beloved family home as well as investment funds. The spouse is still living in the house, but she's the second wife of the grantor and the kids of the first wife never liked her. The grantor, however, loved both his kids and wife #2 very much, and so he wrote into his trust that the wife had life-long financial support for her "care and maintenance," as well as life-long tenancy of the house. Upon her death, both the investment funds and the house revert to the children to be divided equally. Seems fair enough until you realize that the kids are competing for the same money the spouse is using.

Wife #2 is using the money because she needs to live, after all, and the kids can't do anything about that. However, the house is starting to fall into disrepair. It needs a new roof and the plumbing requires an overhaul. Wife #2 could spend $50,000 on repairs of the house, but that comes out of the trust, and she loses interest income on that amount forever because it is now invested in a house which goes to the two children. Of course she's not going to support the decision to repair the house. On the other hand, the kids want to make sure that the house is still sellable when wife #2 dies. They want the repairs done because that's protecting their inheritance.

So what is a trustee to do? If the grantor had looked carefully at the whole situation, he could have written into the trust that "my second wife has a priority interest over other beneficiaries of this trust." This is definitely a value decision and it sets up boundaries around which the trustee can make decisions knowing that he or she is acting in the best interest of the trust. In this instance, the kids are out of luck, but that's the way it's going to be decided. However, if the grantor had written, "I want my home to be maintained and preserved for my children," that would then favor the wishes of the kids.

What I suggest is to look not only at your values in regard to the various main categories of a trust but for each asset as well, especially if that asset is large or a precious family heirloom.

Values Set Boundaries

The most important aspect of spelling out your values is that it provides boundaries within which the trustee can make decisions. The guesswork is taken out of the equation. Having said that, it is also important you define your values in terms that can be implemented. For

> **Technology Teaser**
> The way in which we have set up the computer programs can guide the administrator through the decision process. The program will take a request, relate it to the directives of the trust, and give the administrator guidance in its decision making. It will take a lot of the guess work out of it for the administrator.

example if you want someone to care for your dog in the event of your death, you will obviously want to define what you mean by "care." You don't want to define something so outlandish that it can't be followed. Instead, you want to give clear guidelines. If you have a Cocker Spaniel you may want to define that the standard of care is that set by the published guidelines of the SPCA relating specifically to Cocker Spaniels. You may also want to express that the care is to last the dog's natural lifetime and that another named party is designated to check on the care of the dog periodically to assure compliance. It is also prudent to provide that the supervisor can relieve the caretaker of his or her responsibility for the dog and find another suitable caretaker in the event of the person's inability to properly care for the animal.

Your value boundaries should be enforceable. For example, if you set a value that preventative medicine includes exhaustion of all natural remedies first, you may find it difficult to find an individual or entity that will exhaust your directives before requesting standard medical care. The expression of your values must be relatively simple, universally accepted, and standardized so as to make your trust portable from one trustee to another and from generation to generation. Think about the conditions you place on your beneficiaries and how easy it will be for your administrator to follow. Take for example the trust created by the founder of a major automobile manufacturer. He prohibited his children from traveling in any other type of automobile than the one created by his company. This restriction was imposed for their entire life with the penalty of disinheritance if they failed to comply. While the value is fairly obvious, the ability of the trustee to monitor the comings and goings of the beneficiaries was impossible. It required twenty-four hour surveillance to enforce this provision. In short it was not enforced.

When you see any of the major categories in your trust like "health," "standard of living," "standard of care," in fact any word that can be interpreted in multiple ways by different people, it is important to establish the boundaries around those terms in relation to your values. Technology will do this for us, but for now such specification allows the personal representative guidance and imposes restrictions on decision making. (Here's another, related tip: if you have a living or "Grantor" trust, do not fall into the trap of including broad language for yourself. The broad language drafted to apply to us will carry over to the successor as well, and then you've got big problems.)

You accomplish four things by such specification: 1) you have eliminated the guess work as to what you intend; 2) you have established a standard of care against which performance can be measured; 3) you have set supervisory authority to make sure the standard is met; and 4) you have provided a mechanism for removal if there is abuse. These are value boundaries that will survive for the life of your trust and provide a measure against which performance can be measured.

Values in Action

Now, to show you how this all works together, I'm going to give you an in-depth analysis of the term "education":

Analyze your Values

When you're looking at how you value education, you want to ask yourself some very specific questions (here is where your values play a part in decision making):

Because your representatives act within the boundaries you specify in your trust, the boundaries defined by your values are really constraints you set based on the values you embrace. Let's look at the various constraints you need to consider placed on the category of education:

Value: What is your purpose in providing for benefits for the education of your children or beneficiaries? Is it to support the concept of education in general so funding is available for any level or type of education? Is the goal to grant to each beneficiary at least a college education? Is the goal to foster the ability to support one's self? Is the goal to promote advanced thinking at the graduate level? This is where your goal in creating the instrument starts to be defined.

Time Constraints: Is there a certain time period within which you expect your beneficiary to avail themselves of the trust benefits defined as education or any other benefit? By answering some typical questions, you can direct the window of time in which you believe such benefits should be made available. For example, you could simply fill out something like the following template that I have designed to specify your values in this area. Here's a hint: these are the types of questions included in the templates which will establish your boundaries in the emerging technology:

I direct that funds shall be available under my trust to an authorized beneficiary for educational purposes as follows:

_____ Funds shall be available from the trust to an authorized beneficiary during his/her entire lifetime.

_____ Funds shall be available from the trust to an authorized beneficiary up to age:

_____25 _____30 _____40 _____50 _____60

_____70 _____80 _____other (specify) _____

_____ Funds shall be made available from the trust for the period from

_____ to _____ for the purpose of _____.

There are additional time constraints on the availability of benefits for education under trust which include:

_____

_____

Level of Education: Is there a level of education you will or will not fund? Will the trust pay for private-school education from pre-school through graduate school? Is there a period of time within which degrees should be obtained or is funding forever? In other words, do you want the trust to fund education at age fifty? If not, then specify the level.

Pre-Condition Constraints: Is the gift of funds from the trust conditioned upon actions or conduct of the beneficiary? For example is the beneficiary required to maintain a certain grade point average as a condition of funding? Is the beneficiary required to contribute financially to his/her own education and if so in what form and for what? Are there conditions to *work* during the summer? Are there constraints around the use or abuse of drugs as a condition of funding?

Of course you would need to set up a mechanism for checks and balances to monitor all of the above as well as to fund them.

Type of School Constraint: Is funding from the trust conditioned upon attending a certain type of school? (Military, religious, private, public)

Cost Constraints: How much is the trust authorized to pay for tuition, fees, books, supplies, housing, meals, tutoring, counseling, medical insurance, travel, living allowance, transportation, technology, etc?

Payment Constraints: Are funds to be paid from principal or income? If there are multiple claims on the funds from separate beneficiaries, is there a priority you wish to establish for payment?

Investment Constraints: If you have set a fixed amount aside to cover the education of your children, you want to make sure the funds are there when needed. These would be set forth in your investment constraints linked to your goal of educating your child. Do you want to set parameters for the types of investments you believe will preserve the assets for when they are needed? Investments by the trustee do not always preserve capital. The stock market may plunge leaving insufficient assets to cover the educational need of the named beneficiaries.

What about the fees of administration that will be drained from the fund you have set aside? Fees and poor investments can leave the trust with insufficient assets to meet the intended goal. Make sure you have put in checks and balances to assure your funds are not depleted by these types of losses.

Fiduciary Constraints: Do you want to define the parameters of the trustee's discretion in investing the funds of the trust for the purpose of providing educational or other benefits? Have you set a standard against which the fiduciaries performance can be measured? Have you set up fail-safe provisions to assure fiduciary performance so failed performance is caught early and replacement fiduciaries can take their place? Have you provided a mechanism to catch the loss early enough so the funds have not been depleted by the time you catch the error? Have you anticipated failure of performance? I promote early detection and hold that technology will provide the fail safe.

Priorities for Use of Funds: In addition to the basic parameters of funding, you must also contemplate, anticipate, and plan for the unexpected. Funding may be made available if certain opportunities arise so your child does not lose the advantage of seizing the opportunity. You must also contemplate what benefits will have priority. For example, if you have slated $200,000 to your son for college and he is in a car accident leaving him partially disabled, can the funds be used to assist him in his hospitalization and/or rehabilitation? Your values should be ranked in priority order, e.g. health, education, support, welfare—or however you choose to do it. What's important is you establish the priorities for use of funds. This takes the guess work out of these decisions for your personal representative.

This is a lot to digest and you may be asking yourself if you can anticipate all of this and plan for it. The answer is, yes you can. When the technology becomes available, the capabilities will be almost endless, but remember that it is the standard of performance and boundaries you are establishing for administration. But until that becomes available, it requires work and planning on your part. It is time well spent, however, because it will help ensure that your trust is being handled in the way you intend.

The Rewards of Education

Remember the guy who was working on his fourth doctorate? The grantor who put language in his trust that his son was to be supported by the trust "as long as he remained in school" set in motion a parasitic relationship between the beneficiary and the trust. The child simply became dependent upon the trust and avoided the reality of ever having to support himself by getting a job. The other beneficiaries aren't happy with their errant brother, but the trustee is bound by the language of the trust. He has no choice but to fund this never-ending education because the grantor failed to specify his values on education.

While it is certainly up to you to decide which values you want to espouse, I want to make you aware of the outcomes to some of the decisions that you make. You want your children to be provided for, and you may have all the best intentions in the world. But where does one draw the line between "providing for" a child and helping them get a hand up in life? When I'm asked, I advocate that any funds that are given to the child are done so to help make a child more self-sufficient. Education isn't an end in itself. It should be used to train a person for a profession. Work, in one sense, is an education in and of itself. This means work in the real world where your resume, interview, and skills determine whether you get the job. Here is where your children will learn to depend upon their own skills or lapse back into support by the family. Those who do not have family money have to rely on their own skills for their own support and survival. Those with family money should learn the same lessons, for constant dependency breeds more of the same.

If you support your children forever, they will never have the incentive to generate money for themselves. Life is simply too easy the other way. Structure and educate your children in a plan that gives them a finite amount and a certain end date. Ascribe what the funds are to be used for and stick to it. Articulate to your children that you are providing them the opportunity to be educated. It is a gift that you give them to prepare them for their future. Advise them that the level of education they attain is in direct proportion to the opportunities that will be available to them. (The charts below give you some pertinent information regarding the ratio of education and opportunity.) It is their choice as to how hard they want to work to attain the choices they would like to have.

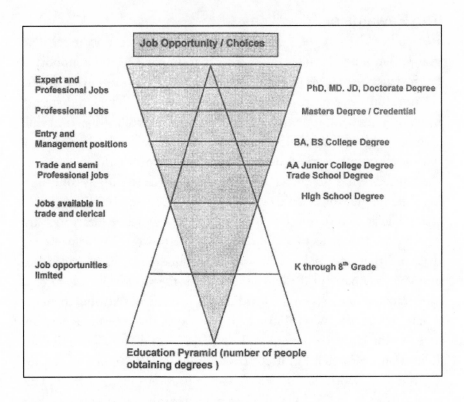

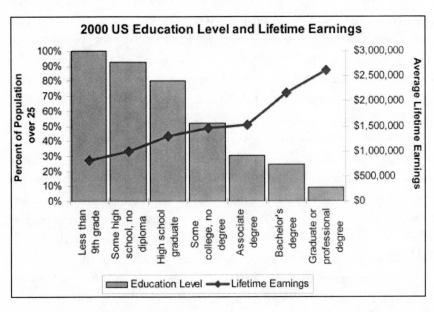

The data is clear. The more education a person has, the more that person is likely to earn. The more they earn, the more apt they are to be self-sufficient. Statistics on the educational level and earnings obtained with different levels of education support the fact that education should absolutely be one of the goals of your trust.

Now having said that, I also realize that there are those who make it on experience alone. They grew up helping in the family business, and they alone know it better than anyone else. This of course is an education in itself and in this case, education might not be an over-riding concern. But not everyone has this type of opportunity provided for by their family, and in today's global market, it's still a good idea to learn about business. In reality, education is often the only way of assuring that your beneficiaries have the building blocks necessary to survive with or without trust money.

Even if you have enough money that your children will never have to work a day in their lives, it is no favor to them to foster a lack of self-esteem by making your children trust-fund babies, dependent upon your wealth. Individual self-worth comes from a person's own accomplishments and struggles to attain his or her own dreams and goals. Whether you have the funds or not, always emphasize to your children that you expect them to become self-supporting. Let them know the education they are being provided and the choices they make should result in their own productiveness and independence. Since you control the purse at this stage, help guide them in their choices. If culinary arts are your son's passion, have him take business courses as well so he understands the restaurant business. If he fails, he has an MBA business background to fall back on. If science is of interest, urge your daughter to strive toward a Ph.D. or medical degree. If political science is intriguing, then direct him or her into the study of government or law. Choices in the arts, dance, painting, sculpture, music, film etc. should also be accompanied by a general business background. Push the MBA program (but don't require it).   Most important, you should clearly explain to each child that this gift is finite. Once the specific limits that you have placed on the gift are reached, there is no more money.

One of my favorite ways of ensuring that the trust really does fund the goal of making a person self-sufficient is to provide ongoing decision making to the beneficiary. First, the partial distributions should be from the same pot from which the education is funded. If you set aside $200,000 for each child, tell them they either have enough to go to Harvard at $50,000 per year (if they get in) or go to a public university and reserve some of the money for graduate school. Or they can do nothing and receive one-half the amount in a lump sum at whatever age you specify. If they do nothing, you can specify that they may be supported by a total of one-half the amount at a rate of whatever dollar figure you specify until whatever age you specify. The balance may or may not be given to them at a specified date, but that is all there is. There will be nothing available to them after it runs out. Whatever they decide to do, the choice is theirs, and while this is just an example, it shows you how a defined window works for the availability of the benefit.

Above all, urge them to reach for the stars. I never advise anyone to set limits on goals to be reached. Always have them strive to be better than they are and to believe that they can accomplish more than they think. Limited or negative thinking has no place here.

One other bit of hard advice that I want to give you is this: do not raise the expectation in your children that they will receive more on your death. (You may or may not be able to—or wish to—provide additional funding but that is your business, not theirs.) This does not mean that you shouldn't talk to your children about your assets, what they expect, and what you expect. I'm not going back on what I have been advocating all along. Rather, this advice comes from many years of watching very wealthy families whose kids think that all the money is going to roll right to them when their parents die. This creates disincentive. If the child's every need is met, then there's no motivation to try to do anything to satisfy his or her own needs. I firmly believe that a child should never expect or even be guaranteed that he or she is going to get the entire estate. To do so promotes a lack of motivation and a dependency on the family money in the trust, and that doesn't do anyone any favors in the long wrong.

When you do talk to your kids, find out not only what they think about your assets but what their goals are in life, what they expect, and what their motivations are. What I'm trying to get you to avoid is leaving your children with too much of a sense of entitlement. They're not stupid. They know the rough value of your home, your jewelry, your art, and whatever other valuable property you have. They can guess how much you make if you haven't told them. But having a sense of entitlement can endanger the trust and your goals. It creates obvious problems for trustee and hurts your children because they quickly become resentful when the benefits are not what they expected. So again, I say, your children should not have the sense that they're going to get everything you have. There's a great story in another book on trusts called *Beyond the Grave*. A very wealthy father told his children that he was going to give them each $300,000 on his death. This changed things drastically for everyone. There was even a divorce because the marriage was based only on the future inheritance.

In the end, it is your money and you can do with it what you want. But I strongly recommend making education a priority. All too often I have seen beneficiaries of wealthy families who are clueless about how to handle the assets they have been left. It is not too long before the funds are squandered, poorly invested, or subject to a con artist's deceptive game and lost altogether. No matter how much or how little you gift to your children, if they are educated to appreciate the gift, they will make better choices and decisions with the assets they receive.

No matter where your values lie, it is important to articulate them in as many specific ways as possible. For it is only with well defined values that a trust administrator is capable of doing the job for which he has been retained.

CHAPTER TEN

Technology: The New Paradigm in Trusts

If your head is spinning from all the information I have given you, I understand. While devising a decent plan for your trust isn't rocket-science, it definitely involves a lot of detail, details that you may not want to confront, let alone deal with every three years—the interval of time that I suggest you revisit your estate plan to ensure that it is up to date.

There is hope, however. Throughout the book, I have been teasing you with various ways emerging technology in the trust and estate arena can help alleviate many of the problems, as well as make their setup and execution far easier and more efficient. With the sophisticated yet workable software that is the basis of this new technology, there is the possibility of transforming an industry that operates as if it were still in the 1600s to an industry that should be responsive to the needs and desires of those it serves. My years of work and research in this field has led me to conclude that the industry has not changed much in the last four-hundred years because the disconnect between all the entities involved is too great. The drafter, professionals, and service providers are split in space and time from each other.

With technology driving the creation of our trusts, a trust will no longer be under the veil of secrecy that shrouds the entire industry. While I have not highlighted this as one of the many problems that plague trusts and trust creation, secrecy certainly contributes to the problems. People tend to think that the problems they suffer are unique to them. It is an industry that is traditionally based on confidential relationships and family money, so when a family runs into trouble, they remain quiet. But the lack of communication over this entire subject has left a vacuum of information and an imposed ignorance by those who benefit from the industry. This general black box where not even our libraries provide a road map as to just how the system works has resulted in: widespread abuse, loss of assets, family hatred and general dysfunction. But because we are all using the trust system because we are accumulating more wealth, it is time to become vocal. *No one* should have to believe that there is nowhere for people to go and no better system available. If we, the consumers, demand better products and services then those who set up and administer our trusts will have to comply.

The only way we can demand this better product is if we incorporate the usable technology advanced computer software gives us into the system. The simple fact is that only by using the power new technology grants to us will the trust industry become more responsive. The benefits of this new technology are almost endless. Just to name a few: technology allows a different model that is better, more accountable, and more responsive to our wishes. As technology emerges in this area, terms used by one person or attorney will mean the same thing from person to person and attorney to attorney. The new technology provides an administrative process that is transparent and accountable. It allows decisions to be made within boundaries set by the grantor and accessed and tracked by the beneficiaries.

The new technology will allow you a new way of designing your trust and or will give you input into the decision made in the future eliminating discretionary decisions made on our behalf giving way to decisions made by us. The decisions will reflect our intent, values, goals, and eliminate broad discretionary decisions that benefit only the personal representative. The technology takes out what I have been calling the "time bombs" in the trust, those hidden decisions that cause the destruction of the trust estate and the family it is to benefit. It is linked to the all-important implementation plan and execution plans that are based on the directives we have outlined in our trust's design. It catches the inconsistencies, the mistakes, the bad decisions, the actions that should not be taken and the conflicts of interest.

And there is something even more exciting about this new technology. It can even help those trusts that are already in motion and currently under management. Once a trust is put in electronic form along with any other amendments, court orders etc., that may change its terms, these trusts too can be mapped into a predictable administrative plan.

A Trust's Real Risk

The idea of a trust really comes down to controlling your wealth and assets, and anytime you give control of your wealth and assets to someone else, you take on a risk that your plan will fail. Just as the professional fiduciaries want to minimize their risks as I've outlined them in chapter 6, both the grantors and the beneficiaries want to ensure as best they can that their plan won't fail. Only when the emerging trust technology becomes widely available will you be able to control and even sharply limit the risk of loss, the risk that your plan will not be implemented, and the risk that even if followed mistakes in its execution won't endanger the trust's assets.

While I've talked at length about the importance of having a good design, implementation, and execution plan, my technologist, Ernest Freeman, with input from Michael Besack, developed mathematical formulas dealing with the risk that impacts the trust and estate world. They were key in helping me recognize the three elements of a trust that everyone must consider, and because of all of our research, we were able to recognize each of the three elements of a trust by the risk they each presented. And while I've gone into depth about each stage of a trust's plan, what we call the "life cycle" of a trust I think it bears repeating the risks associated with each.

Design risk refers to inherent risk attributed to ambiguities, errors, and inconsistencies contained in the trust or will documents themselves. Amendments, evidence of interpretation, court interpretations, etc. all add to this risk. Risk under this category also includes risk associated with the assets of the trust or will, as well as conflicts, ambiguities, inconsistencies in applicable laws, regulations, and policies. There is even risk involved with the beneficiaries because much can happen, both in status and in situation, between the time the trust or will is written and the time the trust or will springs to life.

Implementation risk of the trust or will is inherent in how well the grantor has defined for the trustee how to accomplish what is written in the trust or will. The risk, or lack of it, depends on how well the grantor has been able to answer how decisions are to be made: How are terms defined? How are the goals to be accomplished? What agents are to be employed? What parameters of performance are set? What are the markers of accomplishing the goals? When will a goal be determined accomplished or failed? How are assets to be managed in meeting the goals that have been set? What investments are to be made and when? How are constraints to be applied? How does the administration of the trust or will comply with existing and changing laws, regulations, and policies? How do the beneficiaries access their benefits in a predictable manner? What constraints do they have to overcome before benefits will be made available to them, and what triggers are automatic to get the gifts the grantor intends to the right people at the right time minimizing third-party intervention?

Execution risk refers specifically to whether the plan is properly performed. The risk, or lack of it, is tied to how well the grantor has anticipated the tasks of administration. Has the plan met time deadlines? Have the selected agents performed within the boundaries of their duty, applicable laws and regulations, and within the parameters of the trust? Is ongoing administration maintained at the highest level? Have checks and balances been put in place, and are they operating to assure that the conduct of our personal representatives meet the standards imposed?

Technology Controls Your Risk

Ensuring that you have adequate control over your trust in reality equates to minimizing the risk that your plan will fail, not be implemented, or will be executed badly resulting in a frustration of the goal and loss to your beneficiaries. Any one of the above risks individually or in combination can spiral the assets you leave into partial or total loss.

When we contemplate the number of areas of risk that can negatively impact the bottom line of our estate or trust, it is important to understand the true lack of control we currently have on the outcome of the plan we have made for our assets and families. Our current system of estate planning, administration, and execution is premised on too many conflicting, ambiguous and subjective standards of performance for it to work well in today's society. Indeed it is entirely premised on "trust," trust that our representative will operate with integrity; trust that they will have the acumen and training to do the job; trust that the assets will be preserved as we intended; trust that outside influences and conflicts of interest do not invade or sidetrack decisions over our assets; trust that mistakes will be discovered and corrected; trust that fees and expenses will not consume the gift.

If on the other hand the grantor is able to consistently define the parameters and constraints that may limit the gifts he or she intends to bestow under the trust or will, the areas of ambiguity and risk begin to shrink. If his or her directives are linked to an implementation plan that guides the administrator seamlessly through the administrative process with 70 – 80 percent of the questions already answered by the grantor, again risk is reduced. When risk is reduced the grantor actually accomplishes his or her intended goal, and the heirs become the ultimate beneficiaries of the grantor's intended benefits.

Having seen again and again the inconsistent, subjective, self-serving, and negligent administration of estates and trusts by lay and professional administrators and trustees alike, it occurred to me early on that with the advent of computer technology there must be a better way. Why had the trust and estate industry remained untouched by the technological revolution that was impacting just about every phase of our lives in every other industry? I watched for twenty years anticipating that my job in the trust and estate arena both suing and defending erring trustees would be revolutionized by changes in technology that would guide the trustee and administrator seamlessly through a process that would help them "do it right."

After twenty years of anticipating change and none on the horizon, I concluded that I knew how to guide these estates and trusts through the process so liability could be avoided, the trust assets distributed in a timely manner, and disputes minimized. I realized that if I got the trust early enough, I could ultimately help the beneficiaries avoid up to 90 percent of the problems that emerge by doing it right from the beginning. In order to do this, I knew I would have to find a computer whiz or two to help me see if software and services could be developed to provide parameters for the trustees and estate administrators to follow so that 1) decisions could be made within a "safety zone" and 2) the beneficiaries could be kept happy because all decisions were made in accordance with applicable legal standards. I knew that with technology used well, benefits would become predictable and the highest standard of accountability would be imposed on the whole trust industry. In short, problems would not emerge.

To my great fortune I met and convinced Ernest Freeman to work with me in my quest to empower the individual and family to protect themselves from later dissipation of their assets at the hands of strangers and to develop a system that allowed the chosen representative to be guided through the administrative process as defined by the grantor and applicable law. He is a talented software engineer with thirty years of technology experience in knowledge management systems and system design. He brought in computer-architecture technologist Michael Besack, and we went to work. In our seven-year journey together, we have studied the why's and how's associated with where trusts and estates go wrong and have devised a system that is not only more efficient and cost effective but one that better reflects the goals and wishes of the grantor. To this end, we have discovered more about how we all think, plan, and make decisions, and how we are impacted by culture, history, and our own unique way of looking at our assets and families.

Since I do not believe in the perfect trust or will or the perfect administrator or trustee, I believe that we should "routinize" (make routine) how we draft and implement our wills and trusts making decision by our personal representative predictable and measurable. By "measurable" I mean that we have set a standard in our plan against which our administrator's performance can be measured, and the only way to do this is with sophisticated and workable computer technology—in other words, a new trust technology.

Ernest Freeman with input from Michael Besack have researched and devised software and an architectural structure that provides a solution for trusts that incorporates all the areas that I have talked about in this book. They have developed the architecture for the technology solution that I have been hinting at from the beginning because only with computers will a grantor have the kind of input into the design, implementation, and execution of his or her trusts and estates so his or her wishes are actually executed in a manner consistent with their wishes.

This software and trust architecture also benefits the estate planners as they will have tools to project their client's wishes into the future in a consistent predictable manner assuring that the plan they create has an administrative link. Trust officers will not have to guess at what was intended and will no longer incur the high risk associated with trust administration as 80 percent of the decisions will have been made by the grantor. However, while it is uniform in its approach, it's not a "cookie-cutter" solution. Rather, the grantor chooses the administrative services that fit his or her goals. It is a system that is designed to take you, the grantor, through the decision-making process answering specific questions regarding your family and assets. In short, it gives the grantor more control thus minimizing risk of loss.

Here's the good news: the emerging technology will allow us, along with whatever legal, accounting, and tax advisers we want, to adequately design, implement, and execute our trusts and estates at less cost. You as a grantor will be able to answer questions pertaining to your assets, goals, values, each beneficiary, etc., setting the boundaries of the trust so they can be linked to an implementation plan designed to accomplish your goals and wishes. It will then track a workable investment model based on your input or the input of investment advisors you have chosen and to applicable laws and standards of performance. The emerging technology is a dynamic plan, one that changes with input from you as events in your life, your family and assets change. Above all, it is a model that can incorporate huge amounts of data that can be referenced and cross checked; it can respond to changing conditions and events making life easier for everyone.

Here's the bad news: while we have developed the concept, designed the architecture, and vetted a series of ideas, we have not yet been able to develop the software into usable products and services. It is expensive to do so and we don't personally have the money to do it on our own. The banks and trust industry aren't interested in funding it. They make money the way it is and are in fact invested in keeping your trust and assets under their control. When I made presentations to major banks, I met with comments like: "We make money the way it is." "We know we will get the trust business because there is nowhere else for it to go." "We are not feeling any pain in this area." With this attitude, we, the consumers, are the ones who lose.

So what follows is a glimpse into what emerging technology can do. I want to "wet your whistle" as the old saying goes so that you start thinking in different terms when you plan your trust or estate. I want you to start demanding a better model, more accountability, more transparency, fewer secret decisions, more responsiveness, fewer lawyers and lawsuits, more predictability, more protection of our assets and long term goals, and more protection for our children and families. And maybe there will be an intrepid reader or two who decides to step up and say, "I'll help." We will create a different model. (If you're one of them, visit www.fiduciarytechnologiesinc.com. We will love to hear from you!)

New Technology Lets You Do the Impossible

Why would anyone want to invest in this? Because emerging trust technology lets you step into the future. Through a series of decisions in what Ernest Freeman and I call "decision trees," the grantor can specifically customize the management and distribution of assets to his or her family meeting the goals he or she designates. With this new technology, you are allowed to plan for the expected and for the unexpected.

What we have found is that there are only so many life scenarios that can play out and you can anticipate and plan for about 80 – 85 percent of them. Granted, for the remaining 15 – 20 percent, you will have to rely on the integrity and honesty of your personal representative with guidance from you, but 15 – 20 percent is better than 100 percent reliance. By having more input into future decisions for your assets and family, it lessens the burden of parenting and reliance on your chosen representative. It also makes their job easier as they do not have to guess about what you intended. Liability for decisions made is also lessened. If you choose to educate your children through graduate school, it is you who makes the decision not your personal representative. You set the parameters and boundaries for disbursement of funds. You set the conditions the beneficiary must meet to qualify for the educational benefit. It is not arbitrary. It is not subjective. It is predictable, consistent from representative to representative, and the beneficiaries can rely on it to let them know the conditions they must meet in order to receive benefits.

I have seen a trustee withhold funds for shoes in an effort to demonstrate to the beneficiary who was really in charge of her funds. I have seen beneficiaries denied funds for anything other than tuition where the student spent most of her time working so she could afford to live while she was in school. I have seen instances where the trustee arbitrarily stated that they knew what the term "education" meant and it didn't include a trade school.

Again, it is my belief that people should be empowered to make informed decisions for themselves. Give them the information and their available options, and they will usually choose what is best for them. Above all, I object to "big brother" and the imposition of power and control over others. I ran into this exact issue when I was creating my trust before I went in for spine surgery. My son was under-aged, and I needed to name a guardian. His father was dead, so instead of just guessing, I discussed my dilemma with my son and wrote in my trust options of people from whom he could choose as his guardian. But while I could let him know up-front that immediately upon attaining his majority (age eighteen) I granted him control over his assets with the guardian and two to three others as advisors to guide his decisions, I still feared that no matter how specific I was, I would still subject my son to an overbearing trustee. The lesson in all of this, as always, is to communicate and work with the people you expect to act on your behalf and work with those you designate as beneficiaries to assure that the gifts you bestow actually accomplish your intended purpose. However, were the new technology in this area available to me, I would have had the opportunity not only to structure my estate with the assurance that what I had planned would actually play out as anticipated, but the roles of the advisors and guardian I chose for my son would have been spelled out in more detail thus alleviating my fears.

Above all, the emerging trust technology allows the grantor to easily address contingencies. That is practically impossible in the way trusts and wills are structured today, but very easily done with new technology. Even events that are unlikely and improbable can be addressed, and that will give much better direction to those who are administering your trusts.

What Does This New Technology Look Like?

Have I teased you enough already? Are you chomping at the bit, wanting to find out how this stuff actually works? I don't blame you. It's powerful stuff. Computer software has become extremely sophisticated, so much so that it is able to detect patterns and even solve problems based on patterns and outcome. Emerging trust technology will do this with respect to your trusts and estates.

Take the all important category of values as an example. Right now, it is virtually impossible to incorporate your values into a trust in such a way that can guide your personal or professional representative in the decisions he/she makes. But if a pattern is created as to how decisions are to be made by our representatives with a value set applied to particular assets, beneficiaries, activities, and priorities, then it is fair to say that we have the ability to project our values into the future. With emerging trust technology, we can easily provide the all-important road map for our representatives as to how we expect them to accomplish our goals.

Remember the sample template I showed you in the last chapter concerning your values on education? The program takes what you've checked off and creates a pattern of values from it. All of the value patterns the software creates is premised upon the choices you make with respect to a series of questions about yourselves, your family, and your assets. These patterns set the value system you are comfortable with and then defines the parameters within which decision are to be made. It is customized to the individual and the assets with input coming from the grantor, not third-party strangers. The structure is dependent upon the modules of services and products you want employed. It is also designed to give you questions to answers that will set the stage for later administration, setting boundaries and parameters you define and within which your personal representative is to operate. In this manner trustee discretion (making decisions based on what they think as opposed to what you want) is limited and trustee and beneficiary conduct within certain standards is clearly defined.

Until now the only way we could specify what we really wanted was through letters of instruction. Emerging technology in the trust and estate area allows us to have more input into decisions we would like to make for our families once we are gone. With it, the questions that we never thought to ask have been laid out for us to simply respond to. Through this we project ourselves into the future and leave a legacy of defined choices rather than allowing strangers or distant relatives to impose their values on our beneficiaries.

A Sample

In the first step in the trust software program, you will be directed to answer questions on a template similar to the template example I gave you in the previous chapter. You will check off hypothetical questions that set boundaries for decision making by your administrator. Here's a sample template relating to your definition of personal care when you age. To fill it out, you would simply check off whatever point fits you best and then fill in the blanks where appropriate.

Here's the template:

I want my assets and property to be utilized by my trustee for my own health care, maintenance, and support as follows:

I direct that _____income and then _____principal (including the sale) of my assets in the order set forth below shall be used for my care as set forth herein:

Account #_____ at_____
Account #_____ at_____

_____

_____

These shall be used by my personal representative to:

_____Maintain me in my own home at

_____ for as long as I shall live;

____Provide in home care as necessary to maintain me in my home.

____Transfer me to the following nursing and/or residential care facility at age ____80____90____100____110 ____as my doctor (name_____) deems necessary. At this facility, I want to have a ____bedroom; ____I want a personal bathroom ____access to outside, other _____.

____Transfer me to live at _____
     with _____

____Transfer me to hospice for end of life issues
     (name_____).

____I have executed a living will that explains how I wish to be treated regarding end of life care.

I have defined the term "support" in letters of instruction which are incorporated herein.

The term "support" shall include payment from the trust for:

Housing which shall include but not be limited to:

____Care of personal residence of grantor:
____rent
____taxes
____insurance
____maintenance repair
____reconstruction
____improvements
____utilities
____garbage
____other _____

Residential Care or Nursing Home:

____Fees and charges of care facility
____extra-activity fees
____drivers
____taxi's,
____transportation
____entertainment

_____movers
_____Personal nursing
_____Other _____

I have defined the term "health" in letters of instruction and my living will which are incorporated herein

The term Health shall include payments from the trust for:

_____Health insurance
_____Uncovered medical bills
_____Homeopathic medication or treatment
_____Payment of a personal assistant to oversee payments and applications for benefit
_____Emergency care and services

_____I ask my personal representative to avail my trust of all available government benefits so as to preserve trust assets.

Priority of Claims Against Trust.

I list in order of priority the payment of funds with respect to my own care:

_____health care
_____support
_____travel

While these questions are not complete they constitute just a small sample of the questions you would be considering in the preparation of your will or trust, I hope you see that by simply checking them off and filling in the blanks as called for, you will be directing your personal representative in your own care. Here's the neat part. This is just the beginning of what happens. Your responses set boundaries for decision making. This gets integrated into your health directives, your investment plan, your decision tree I mentioned earlier. It is a flow chart that allows the computer program to ultimately tell you whether or not an investment the trustee wants to make works within the parameters you set or whether or not a beneficiary's request can be met.

The Decision-Tree Model

If you've ever worked with a flow chart, you know that the boxes represent various tasks or commands and the arrows represent the flow of information. This is how the decision-tree model in emerging trust technology works:

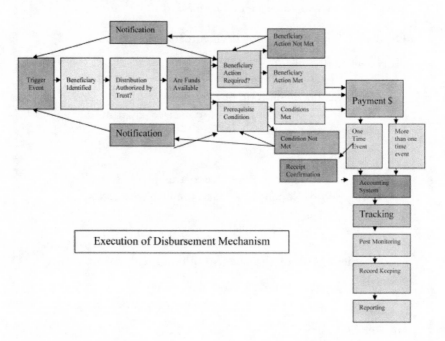

Execution of Disbursement Mechanism

This particular decision tree is specifically for the execution of disbursements from the trust. There are other decision trees for all the other major tasks in a trust. How this particular tree works is quite fascinating. Take the "Are Funds Available" box. The data in this box comes from the information you checked off on various templates ranging from the trust's goals and your values to your assets and everything having to do with them. From this data, there's a whole subset of tasks that the computer will analyze depending on the types of assets that are available. It will consider such things as, are the assets liquid? (Can the trustee get to them fast?) Are there competing interests for the assets or are they clean? (You may have a partnership and so the asset may be much more difficult to liquidate than a stock.) Are there competing claims on the asset? (Is the wife living in the house the trustee has to sell?) The program goes through an in-depth analysis just for this one particular box. Once it decides everything is a go, it then goes to the next decision box and performs the same analysis on that task. It will go from one box to the next until it has gone through the entire decision tree for the trust document.

But the analysis doesn't end there. Once you get the okay from the trust side, then it goes through a whole new process of deciding whether or not the request is legal. This part gets me really excited because the computer program not only thoroughly searches the trust, it also overlays all of the information from the trust with the all the possible legal constraints. For example, it will find out if the request complies with the Patriot Act. (If the beneficiary lives anywhere outside of the United States, there are all sorts of cash constraints.) It will ensure that the request stays within the bounds of Sarbanes Oxley (the Securities and Exchange Commission rules put into place after the Enron debacle of 2001). The computer program will also contain all the probate rules, tax rules, and whatever other applicable laws that are pertinent to trusts and estates *and* not only for the United States but eventually for any country that is pertinent to the beneficiaries. So say you have a beneficiary in South America. If you sent the money to her directly, the government may have all sorts of rules regarding the distribution of that money. While the beneficiary is qualified in terms of the trust to receive the money, the money can be held up by the government or may even be taxed. Not only would the program reference a whole series of international laws and alert the trustee to them, it would also tell the trustee how best to handle that request.

Finally, once the program has gone through the entire process of checking and cross-checking the entire trust and all applicable laws, it approves, or not, the request. If the request is approved, the computer then goes through the process confirming, with trustee input whether the check was cut, received, and recorded (the same process I outlined in chapter 7 in the subsection on execution plans.) This entire process from the first request to the final report is actually the process that should be followed when a request for distribution is made no matter if you have to do it manually or electronically. However, if you have the program in place, doing it electronically takes minutes instead of days, weeks, or even months. Plus you have a computer trail of decisions made, compliance with applicable laws, analysis of the trust instrument and in short a transparent, reliable and repeatable process. Sounds interesting? If you've ever had to deal with a trust that isn't working, I suspect that this is especially exciting. But, again, here's the bad news. While the architecture of the program has been developed, the actual programs have yet to be completed because they need to be funded. (And again, if any of you are now chomping at the bit to help, please let me know at www.suefarley.com or www.fiduciarytechnologiesinc.com.) Emerging technology *will* dramatically change what we may expect; we just need to find a way to put it into place!

The Current System

Now that you have a taste of what the emerging trust technology can do, let me go back to how it is handled now to show you the difference. The current system only allows the tracking of the funds and does little to analyze the trust and its requirements to determine whether a distribution should be made and why. When a beneficiary makes a request for distribution, it may go first to the trust officer who in turn may send the request up for committee review. This requires someone to check the trust document in the file drawer for authority for the distribution and then an internal review is undertaken to determine whether the trust authorizes the distribution and whether there are sufficient liquid assets to meet the demand and further whether there is authority to protect the professional from liability for the requested distribution. If there is ambiguity, the ambiguity must be resolved. All in all this process can take anywhere from five to thirty days or longer. The actual determination of whether to make a distribution may ultimately fall to the "discretion" of the trust officer and whatever procedure or processes he/she/it chooses to employ. And, as is often the case, as the fiduciary exercises his/her/its discretion, the distribution may be denied with no further explanation.

Which would you prefer?

Technology Will Make the System Better

In the electronic world discretionary distributions are a thing of the past. The grantor has authorized the distribution or he hasn't. In such event the trustee simply plays by the laws of the state and the directives of the implementation plan. The execution process provides the requisite checks and balances to assure that the event which has been triggered receives an adequate response in a timely manner. Delays are unnecessary as the trust document has already been scanned and processed for permission and the assets checked for available funds. This type of mechanism tracks the decisions behind the numbers. The above example is just one in a thousand event-tracking mechanisms that can be electronically implemented to assure a complete and accurate history of decision making, due diligence, and circumstances at the time so second guessing later about an earlier decision is kept to a minimum.

Benefits for the Trustee

While this short section might not be of interest to those of you who are faced with creating or modifying your existing estate plan or trust, it should interest the professional trustee very much. The new technology being developed will alleviate much of the liability and a huge amount of risk that any trustee faces. Technology will facilitate the role of the trustee by providing for more input by the grantor and more accountability by the trustee or administrator. Accountings and reports are required annually and decision making by the trustee is made within boundaries set by the grantor. With emerging technology, the grantor will have anticipated and addressed 80 percent of the decisions that have to be made relieving the personal representative of responsibility for them. The new trust technology will neutralize the position of the personal representative. No longer will they sit with absolute authority as they control your assets; rather they will truly be an administrator, simply following the directives of the trust.

Technology Standardizes a Trust

The trust or estate is really nothing more than a mechanism to transfer assets from one party to another. If this transfer is viewed from the perspective of creating goals and mapping of mechanisms to accomplish those goals, the transfer of assets is exponentially simplified. Trusts were originally set up in feudal times in order to protect an estate from having to pay "homage"—taxes basically—to the king. Medieval kings were notoriously unpredictable and would levy huge taxes to support the king and his holdings. We are no longer dealing with that mentality. Instead we have taxing requirements that are predictable and can be mapped against our goals of maximizing the benefits that go to our heirs and not third parties. If we map the goal in the original will or trust and then link it to a process that is defined by applicable standards and procedures for accomplishing those goals, the input of third parties and discretionary authority is eliminated by 80 – 90 percent. If the computer program sets up a decision tree as to how we want our assets to be handled under certain circumstances, we can anticipate events and plan for them. It takes much of the guesswork out of decision making, and as I've been saying all along, I would rather make the decisions about my assets for my family than have a third party do it for me.

The implication of "personal trust" is that each is unique and requires "personal" handling. While there are admittedly very large and complex trusts than can be considered unique, the vast majority of personal trusts are far from unique. Most personal trusts are composed of parts that come from a well known and relatively small set of standard components and activities. While the set of possible events that might occur in a single given trust might seem difficult to predict, the set of possible events that can occur in *any* trust are known and constitute a relatively small set.

To put this idea in numeric perspective: you can look at each of the millions of existing personal trusts as being unique and each requiring a unique administrative action, or see that the totality of trusts consists of components and activities numbering in the 100's, and the possible events that can occur is also on the order of 100's. The power of abstraction works in this way: by recognizing the similarity of trust components and activities and abstracting them into common classes in a process called "resolution," one can build a rather compact library of standard parts and actions. Then any trust can be logically reconstructed using this library. This library maps the entire trust space: the set of all possible trust structures and actions.

Since inception the trust world has been so focused on "personal" service that it has failed to map out and organize the trust space and develop an appreciation of the power of abstraction. To draw on a similarity: at one time most homes built in the United States were truly unique just as when trusts were only used by the very wealthy, they could be unique. But today almost every new home is simply a combination of very standard design components. That doesn't mean that all houses look the same. Your trust will be personalized to you just as any house has its own unique features even though it is still based on a very standard model.

In short, the uniqueness of trusts is not all that unique, but by standardizing the trust process, the role of the trustee can be broken down so that technology can be introduced into the administrative process. In this regard truly personalized service can be provided. The capability of audit controls, of checks and balances, and of monitoring performance for quality and legal compliance becomes possible.

My Plea

In 1984, standing in front of that courtroom in San Francisco, I never imagined that I would have spent a large part of my professional life having to deal with the myriad of problems that plague the trust industry. I sometimes still can't believe the problems I run into, and I can't help but think, every day, that so much of what I see is preventable. The money these people have to spend paying me could be spent on their families—if the person who set up the trust would have known what I know now.

Your money should benefit you, your children, and your heirs. Instead, because the system is set up so badly and those that benefit by the bad setup and management profit so considerably, you and those you love end up the losers. I truly believe that it will only take one bank or trust company to adopt a different model. That can be an existing entity or an entirely new one. Until that happens, however, we as consumers can demand—through the way we write our trusts and the way we plan our estate—more accountability and more responsiveness in the way our trusts are administered.

Once the new system is unveiled, it will transform how we plan our estates and trusts; it will also change how those we name as administrators and trustees take care of our assets and our families. The new trust technology will better protect everything having to do with a trust. In a way, it's like oil. It's taken us thirty-five years to figure out that we shouldn't be dependant upon Middle Eastern oil for our energy. We are now pushing the car companies to develop alternative-fuel vehicles, but it's taken all those years to effect change because too many people were invested in keeping the status quo because they made money the way it was.

The trust and estate industry has not changed because those invested in the current system make money the way it is. We and our families lose because we have no where else to go. We are subject to whatever fees and charges are imposed; we are dependent upon strangers and an untrustworthy system. On the positive side, my partners and I at Fiduciary Technologies Inc. know how to fix it. Once the new technology is put into place, a whole new service industry will evolve with new accountability, predictability, and trustworthiness that is so lacking in the current system. To take a concept from Thomas Allen: when we begin to reflect upon the current system and search diligently for answers to protect what we hold most dear, we will become wise masters directing our energies and thoughts toward the common goal of making the system better for everyone.

Begin by demanding a better model of trusts and more accountability from our trustees. Demand that you get an electronic copy of your trust so you will be ready to use the new technology when it is released. Remember all we need is one bank to do it differently and we will never retreat to the poor model that currently exists. It's sort of like the ATM machine. Why would we ever want to return to standing in line for hours waiting for the bank to give us our money now that we can just pop in our card, get our money, and go?

Disaster-proofing our estate plans is our responsibility. The emergence of technology so long in coming to the field of trusts and estates will allow us to shape our trusts and estates in a manner that